Congressional Studies Series
Ronald M. Peters, Jr., General Editor

CONGRESS AND DEFENSE SPENDING

Congress and Defense Spending

THE DISTRIBUTIVE POLITICS OF MILITARY PROCUREMENT

Barry S. Rundquist

Thomas M. Carsey

University of Oklahoma Press : Norman

Library of Congress Cataloging-in-Publication Data

Rundquist, Barry.
   Congress and defense spending: the distributive politics of military
procurement / Barry S. Rundquist, Thomas M. Carsey.
      p. cm. — (Congressional studies series; v. 3)
   Includes bibliographical references and index.
   ISBN 0–8061–3402–X (alk. paper)
      1. United States—Armed Forces—Procurement.   2. United States—
   Armed Forces—Appropriations and expenditures.   3. United States.
   Congress.   I. Carsey, Thomas M., 1966–   II. Title.   III. Series.

   UC263 .R86 2002
   355.6'212'0973—dc21
                                                              2001053464

Congress and Defense Spending: The Distributive Politics of Military Procurement is Volume 3 in the Congressional Studies Series.

1 2 3 4 5 6 7 8 9 10

CONTENTS

FIGURES AND TABLES

FIGURES

TABLES

ACKNOWLEDGMENTS

This study has benefited from the extraordinary cooperation over a ten-year period of several faculty members and graduate students at the University of Illinois at Chicago (UIC). Barry Rundquist had been teaching courses on distributive politics for a number of years when, in the early 1990s, several graduate students expressed interest in writing dissertations on the problem. Uma Sharma got the ball rolling with her dissertation on military subcontracting. A project by Ittipone Tunyavong and our colleague Rowan Miranda on distributive politics in Chicago (1995) also stimulated our thinking in the early 1990s. The present project started with Jungho Rhee's dissertation on military procurement spending in the United States. Jungho, along with Jeong-Hwa Lee and Rundquist, worked on the logic of a pooled cross-section analysis of defense spending data and produced several papers and journal articles (Rundquist, Lee, and Rhee 1996; Rundquist et al. 1997). Ching-Jyuhn Luor wrote his dissertation under Rundquist's direction and, with Lee, produced papers based on the data set assembled and published by Kenneth Bickers and Bob Stein (1991). When Tom Carsey came to UIC, he too was conscripted by Rundquist to work on distributive politics. Together we have conducted several studies and have supervised dissertations by Lisa Schmit on the relationship of defense contracting and electoral outcomes and by Sabri Samari on logrolling in the House Banking and Currency Committee. To work with such talented people on a day-to-day basis for such an extended period has been a privilege and great fun.

This project has received considerable support from UIC. The Office of Social Science Research and the Campus Research Board have provided seed grants and office space. The Great Cities Institute provided Rundquist with research assistance, office space, and a year off from teaching. The university gave Rundquist a sabbatical leave. The Institute of Government and Public Affairs supported Carsey and provided research assistance for a related study of federal procurement in Illinois. The Summer Research Opportunity Program made it possible for several undergraduates to work on our project, and the political science department provided general support and encouragement. The National Science Foundation (Grant SES-9809370) supported a larger study that we are currently working on that compares the geographic distribution of military procurement spending with federal health, agriculture, transportation, and crime spending. Finally, Marilyn Getsov has helped us to manage the grants and graduate students.

The research assistants on our project have been Sharon Fox, Ching-Jyuhn Luor, and Lisa Schmit. Lisa has been invaluable in helping to gather, merge, manage, and analyze the large data sets that underlie this study.

We have also had good advice from a number of our colleagues in the discipline. Bob Stein and Ken Bickers have generously shared data and advice from the beginning. Ken Mayer shared a data set with us that, although it did not end up in this study, allowed us to explore related questions about military procurement spending. Andrew McFarland, Ashish Sen, Gerald Strom, and John Gardiner served on a number of distributive politics dissertation committees and were continually supportive. Rundquist also thanks John Ferejohn for discussions long ago and occasionally since that continue to pique his interest in distributive politics.

Finally, we thank our wives and families for putting up with us while we do distributive politics. Rundquist thanks Andrea Friedman and Bridget, Matthew, and Abigail, who had the experience up close, and Alicia, Johanna, and Carolyn, who viewed it from a (no doubt) pleasant distance. Carsey thanks his wife, Dawn, and their children, Simon and Jane. Our families' love, support, and understanding provide the bedrock for all that we do, and it is to them that this book is dedicated.

CONGRESS AND DEFENSE SPENDING

CHAPTER ONE

Introduction and Statement of Problem

This book is about an anomaly in political scientists' understanding of congressional policy making. Distributive politics theory, which has been called the dominant theoretical approach to congressional politics (Krehbiel 1991), purports to account for the geographic distribution of the benefits of any policy that is paid for from general tax revenues and can be subdivided easily and allocated piece by piece to different claimants. Distributive politics theory suggests that to get reelected, members of Congress (MCs) organize Congress and create and implement policies so that they can better direct benefits to their constituencies. Different versions of distributive politics theory focus on different institutional structures and behavioral patterns, such as standing committees, political parties, ideological blocs, and a norm of universalism, that are postulated to enable MCs to benefit their constituencies. Most scholars assume that at least from a national perspective, the policy that results from distributive politics is ineffective in addressing societal problems and an inefficient way of allocating societal resources.

The anomaly, one that has existed for more than thirty years, addressed in this study is that military procurement policy, one of the largest and most divisible American public policies, has repeatedly been found *not* to reflect the benefit distribution patterns suggested by distributive politics theory. Theodore Lowi argued that military procurement policy should be distributive:

> But politics works in the short run, and in the short run certain kinds of government decisions can be made without regard to limited resources. Politics of this kind are called "distributive," a term first coined for nineteenth century land policies, but easily extended to include most contemporary public land and resource policy; rivers and harbors ("pork barrel") programs, *defense procurement* and R & D; labor, business, and agricultural "clientele" services; and the traditional tariff. Distributive policies are characterized by the ease with which they can be disaggregated and dispensed unit by small unit, each unit more or less in isolation from other units and from any general rule. "Patronage" in the fullest meaning of the word can be taken as a synonym for "distributive." These are policies that are virtually not policies at all but are highly individualized decisions that only by accumulation can be called policy. They are policies in which the indulged and the deprived, the loser and the recipient, need never come into direct confrontation. Indeed, in many instances of distributive policy, the deprived cannot as a class be identified, because the most influential among them can be accommodated by further disaggregation of the stakes. (1964: 690; emphasis added)

Extending Lowi's work, James Q. Wilson (1973) developed a two-by-two table that categorizes types of public policy based on whether the benefits of a policy and its costs are distributed narrowly or broadly. In Wilson's typology, military procurement policy would be a policy with narrowly distributed benefits and diffuse costs.

The anomaly is that, contrary to Lowi's and Wilson's predictions, a series of studies of military procurement spending during the past thirty-five years have found no clear evidence of distributive effects. What this implies is arguable. One view is that, given its size, if military procurement policy does not evidence distributive politics, then the theory of distributive politics itself should be called into question. Another view is that distributive politics may explain some policies, such as agriculture, but military procurement policy is exceptional, requiring a different explanation of how these expenditures are distributed. During the cold war, a number of scholars argued that military procurement policy is too important to the strategic needs of the national defense for distributive politics to affect it. Thus whether military procurement policy evidences distributive politics has implications for understanding both congressional policy making during the cold war and the nature of policy making in democratic governments.

We argue that the conclusion that distributive politics does not characterize military procurement policy should be questioned because the research on which it is based suffers from several limitations. Since the 1960s scholars have tried to evaluate distributive theories by examining the aggregate level of military procurement expenditures in constituencies across the United States. It is this body of research that forms the basis for political scientists' conclusion that military procurement policy is an anomaly vis-à-vis distributive theory. Yet, as we will show, this research has been inadequate to the task.

This book reports on a new study designed to test distributive theories of military procurement spending. The study is based on an analysis of fifty states over thirty-five years. We develop a more complete theory of distributive politics, and we employ a more appropriate statistical modeling approach compared to previous studies.[1] We explore the extent of congressional influence on the targeting of military procurement expenditures, what form the congressional influence takes, and the effect of the distributive politics of military procurement spending on national defense policy and local economic conditions.

A reasonable question is why a research approach other than the statistical analysis of the geographic distribution of military procurement data is not used to study distributive politics in

Congress. First, establishing an evidentiary base for a conclusion about distributive politics in any policy area is difficult. If one chooses to conduct elite interviews, who does one interview? Opponents of a policy tend to label it "pork barrel," a waste of the public's money. Proponents of the same policy and the administrators charged with carrying it out tend to justify it as an important public good. When one balances the views of proponents and opponents, as journalistic norms require, it is unclear what conclusions can be reached. Second, scholarly case studies of how decisions about particular weapons systems are made and how contracts for developing and producing these weapons are distributed face the same interviewee bias problem. It is also questionable whether one can discern a general conclusion about distributive politics from all the detailed information available about the complex, multiyear process of deciding to try to build a particular weapon and implementing that decision (King, Keohane, and Verba 1994). One may get a good description of the process involved (e.g., Sapolsky's *The Polaris System Development* [1972]) and probably which MCs' constituencies had contractors, but to evaluate distributive theories, one needs to compare the constituencies that got the contracts with those that did not. Moreover, when one concludes a study of a particular weapons system, one knows only about that system, and it is difficult to extrapolate from a specific case to the general practice in this multibillion-dollar policy area.

In this book we discuss various versions of distributive politics theory and the current state of the evidence on them. We show that there is considerable disagreement in the political science literature about the nature of distributive politics generally. The only consensus is that distributive politics is not a part of the congressional policy making that produces military procurement policy. However, we show that there are problems in the conceptualization and design of the research that underlies this consensus.

BACKGROUND

Since World War II the Department of Defense (DOD) has spent well over $10 trillion adjusted for inflation (e.g., Crump and Archer 1993: 42), about half of which has been attributed directly to the U.S.-Soviet cold war (Huntington 1961; Kaufman 1992). Annually, defense spending has ranged between $200 billion and $300 billion (in constant 1988 dollars). Defense spending, measured as a percent of gross domestic product (GDP), declined from about 40 percent in 1944 and 1945 to 14 percent in 1952 and about 5 percent in 1992 (Dawson and Stan 1995: 16). Many would argue that the costs of defense spending in terms of forgone alternative spending—both by individuals and corporations that could have paid lower taxes, consumed more private sector goods and services, and invested more in capital formation and by federal, state, and local governments that could have spent the same tax revenues to accomplish other goals—have been enormous.[2]

About one third of defense spending has been for military procurement and research and development (RDT&E). Military procurement spending has declined from about 5 percent of GDP in the early 1950s to less than 1 percent in the 1970s and to even less in the 1990s. It rose to almost 2 percent during the Reagan administration buildup in the 1980s. As a percentage of total DOD spending, procurement has ranged from nearly 40 percent in the early 1950s to a low of about 20 percent in the mid-1970s and back to about 30 percent in the 1980s and 1990s. Not surprisingly, procurement spending has been higher during armed conflicts such as Korea and Vietnam (Dawson and Stan 1995: 19).

National security is a classic public good: it is too costly and unwieldy for individuals to provide for themselves, and it is impossible to exclude individuals from enjoying it once it is provided. Some argue that such public goods tend to be underprovided, because individuals have incentives not to contribute to them, although Sandler and Hartley (1995) point out that bureaucratic efforts to sustain and expand programs and their budgets counter-act the pressure toward underprovision. Because it is a public good, however, governments must use their coercive powers to obtain the revenue necessary to provide for the national defense. Sandler and Hartley (1995) report that most models designed to predict a country's level of defense spending consider the size of a nation's economy, typically measured as GDP.[3] Another impor-tant factor can be the level of defense spending by a country's allies, as countries that are members of an alliance may be able to rely on other members' defense expenditures. Levels of national defense spending also respond to the degree of perceived threat, typically measured as the level of defense spending by enemy or rival countries. Focusing specifically on the superpower rivalry between the United States and the former Soviet Union during the cold war, McGinnis and Williams (2001) find that each country's level of defense spending responds quickly to changes in the levels spent by the other. Their analysis also shows that levels of defense spending depend on each country's preexisting trend.

This book is *not* about predicting the *level* of military procure-ment spending in the United States. For the most part we take the level of military procurement spending as given, although in chap-ter 8 we consider the impact of varying military procurement budget levels on the occurrence of distributive politics. Once the level of expenditure has been determined and the revenue raised, how-ever, the government has a pool of money to spend. We analyze the decision-making process on where this money is spent, focus-ing specifically on *changes* in the subnational geographic distribu-tion of those funds. What the national government chooses to buy and from whom can benefit some places more than others. More-over, because everyone must pay taxes, these benefits come at the expense of individuals and corporations that have paid for, but do not receive, defense procurement contracts. By controlling for the national level of defense procurement spending, our analysis allows us to focus on factors that influence change in the subnational geo-graphic distribution of defense benefits.

The political problem involved in the allocation of billions of dollars of military procurement funds is twofold: How can government obtain the goods and services required to provide for the national defense? And how can individuals and localities get at least enough defense procurement expenditures to make up for what they pay in taxes to support the common defense? The two goals may, of course, conflict. The best bombs, missiles, and aircraft may be built in one or a few cities, and everyone else may have to pay. Or defense benefits may be spread out so that both the national defense is provided for and many localities benefit. The role of congressional politics in resolving conflicts between these two goals is the subject of this book.

GEOGRAPHIC DISTRIBUTION OF
DEFENSE CONTRACTING

Throughout the postwar period, defense spending generally and military procurement spending in particular have tended to be geographically concentrated. For example, Crump and Archer (1993) report that 75 percent of defense expenditures have been received by only ten states. Figure 1.1 presents four maps of the United States showing the distribution of per capita military procurement awards, adjusted for inflation. For four years selected from our 1963 to 1995 period, the maps show the level of per capita military procurement expenditures allocated to states divided into quartiles.[4]

The figure suggests three conclusions. First, at any one time there is substantial inequality in the distribution of military procurement expenditures per capita across states. States in the highest quartile typically receive at least four times as much in military procurement awards per capita than those in the lowest quartile and often twice as much or more than states in the second quartile. Of course, depending on a state's population, the per capita amounts used to establish these rankings may translate into differences between states in total military procurement spending of hundreds of millions of dollars.

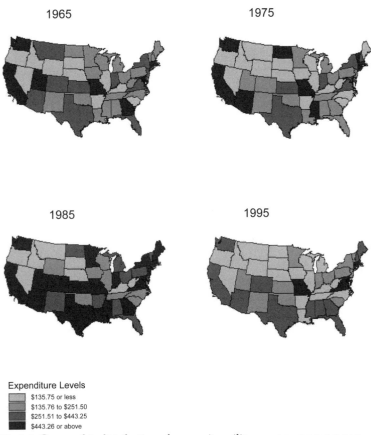

Fig.1.1. Geographic distribution of per capita military procurement expenditures, selected years.

Second, there is a balance between stability and change in which states tend to receive more military procurement awards per capita than others. Some states, such as Massachusetts, Connecticut, Missouri, and California, consistently rank in the highest quartile, while others, such as Nebraska, Illinois, and Kentucky, are typically in the lowest quartile. However, the relative fortunes of some states, including Colorado, Maine, and Louisiana, appear to vary from 1965 to 1995.

Third, more states were ranked in the middle two quartiles in 1965 than in any of the subsequent years shown in figure 1.1. This suggests an increasing polarization in the geographic distribution of military procurement expenditures in the last third of the twentieth century.

The degree of stability or change in the geographic distribution of military procurement funds is also reflected by the correlation between the relative levels of defense contracting in states at different points in time (Crump and Archer 1993). Table 1.1 reports the simple Pearson correlation coefficients relating the level of per capita military procurement awards distributed across states for the same years covered by figure 1.1.[5]

Table 1.1 shows four things. First, the correlation between the distribution of procurement awards among states over time is generally higher when the time period considered is shorter. The correlations covering ten-year intervals range from .63 to .79, while two of the three correlations covering longer periods are about .42. We also see a weaker correlation between the distribution of military procurement contracts in 1995 and 1965 than between 1995 and either 1975 or 1985. This indicates a considerable change in the relative distribution of procurement awards across states over this thirty-year period. Still, the presence of even a moderate correlation ($r = .41$) stretching across a thirty-year period is testimony to the inertia present in the distribution of military procurement awards. Some of the original relative positioning among states in 1965 is still evident thirty years later, even after the Vietnam war, the Reagan buildup, and the end of the cold war.

Second, table 1.1 shows that significant change in the geographic distribution of military procurement awards takes place over time. Even though many of the correlations are fairly high, squaring those correlations to calculate the proportion of the variance in one year's distribution that is explained by the distribution a decade or more earlier shows that much of each year's distribution of defense expenditures remains unexplained. For example, although the correlation between the distribution of procurement awards between 1975 and 1985 is .77, when squared, we find that only about 60 percent of the variance in the geographic distribution of

TABLE 1.1.

Pearson Correlation Coefficients for the Geographic Distribution of Per Capita Military Procurement Contracts across the Fifty States, Selected Years

	Per Capita Contracts, 1965	Per Capita Contracts, 1975	Per Capita Contracts 1985	Per Capita Contracts, 1995
Per capita contracts, 1965	1.00	.791	.862	.411
Per capita contracts, 1975	.791	1.00	.773	.427
Per capita contracts, 1985	.862	.773	1.00	.631
Per capita contracts, 1995	.411	.427	.631	1.00

NOTE: $N = 50$ for each correlation coefficient. Military procurement contract awards are measured as per capita dollars and adjusted for inflation.

defense procurement in 1985 can be accounted for by knowing the distribution ten years earlier. That leaves 40 percent of the variance to be explained by other factors. Similarly, slightly less than 17 percent of the variance in the distribution of military procurement expenditures across states in 1995 can be explained by the distribution of military procurement expenditures in 1965. Another way to read this book is as a study of the political dynamics that account for the transition from the initial distribution of military procurement expenditures observed in the early 1960s to that observed in 1995.

Third, the most recent decade is characterized by relatively substantial change. The three weakest correlations reported in the table all involve the 1995 distribution. The correlation of .63 between 1995 and 1985 is substantially lower than the ten-year correlations between 1965 and 1975 (.79) and 1975 and 1985 (.77). Thus it appears that the extent of the inertia in the distribution of military procurement expenditures lessened at the end of the cold war.

Fourth, the highest bivariate correlation presented is between 1965 and 1985. This suggests that the buildup during the early years of the Reagan administration may have been concentrated in some of the same states that were relatively advantaged during the early phases of the Vietnam war. In contrast, the relatively low correlation between 1975 and 1995 suggests that the distributions of military procurement awards that result during periods of declining defense spending are less related.

Scholars have tended to disagree about the nature and causes of the geographic distribution and concentration of military procurement expenditures. Economists have emphasized the concentration of economic capacity and have tended to lament that defense contracting is more dispersed than it should be vis-à-vis capacity. They generally blame congressional politics for this (e.g., Peck and Scherer 1962; Gansler 1981; Wolf 1988). In contrast, some political scientists contend that congressional politics does *not* influence military procurement policy making (e.g., Goss 1972; Mayer 1991). Even among political scientists who see a role for congressional politics, agreement has not been reached on whether committee representation, partisanship, the ideological orientations of MCs, or the norm of universalism is a more important factor.

In sum, there is considerable cross-sectional and intertemporal variation in the state-by-state distribution of military procurement expenditures. Our question is whether distributive politics in Congress can account for it.

DISTRIBUTIVE POLITICS

Theories of distributive politics focus on how the reelection goal of MCs combines with the organizational structure of legislative policy making to affect the geographic distribution of policy benefits. Distributive theories can be thought of as theories about how MCs try to solve the collective action problems associated with making policy (distributing benefits) in a way that facilitates their reelection. Shepsle and Bonchek (1997) argue that distributive politics, as defined by Lowi, inherently induces cycles in voting coalitions under majority rule. They say that distributive politics can be represented as a simple "divide-the-dollar" game, for which there is no Condorcet winner (see also Baron and Ferejohn 1989). In lay terms, this means that, absent some institutional structure to impose an equilibrium solution of some sort, no stable voting majority will be able to form around distributive policy making. Of course, the observable world shows that endless voting cycles do not occur in allocating defense procurement or other distributive policies (Tullock 1981). Instead, rules, norms, or, more generally, an institutional structure provides some stability to distributive policy making. The relevant conclusion, then, as Shepsle and Bonchek point out, is that the final outcomes of distributive politics are sensitive to the various institutional features of congressional decision making. The distributive theories we explore in this volume deal explicitly with such institutional features as partisan and ideological divisions, bicameralism, and the committee structure of Congress.

Distributive theories focus on the dynamics of the policy-making process, yielding predictions about the factors that might influence

changes in the geographic distribution of policy benefits. They por-
tray MCs as trying to create and influence the various internal institutional structures in Congress to facilitate pursuit of their goals.
However, because they are difficult to change, or at least difficult to
change quickly, once established, such structures are not wholly
endogenous to policymaking. Here we provide a brief sketch of the
various versions of distributive theory that we examine in this book.

A committee-centered version of distributive theory argues that
the local beneficiaries of defense spending will be individuals, corporations, and communities located in states or congressional districts whose MCs sit on a defense committee in Congress (e.g.,
Shepsle, Weingast, and Johnson 1981; Weingast and Marshall 1988).
MCs from areas that do defense contracting seek membership on
the military committees so that they can maintain or increase the
current level of defense contracting in their constituencies in order
to win votes on election day. Party leaders, who control the committee assignment process, tend to grant the committee requests
of party members in order to increase the members' chances of
reelection and thus their own likelihood of remaining or becoming
the majority party in their chamber. Once they are on a military
committee, MCs tend to use their position to advantage their constituencies, either directly by authorizing or funding projects or
indirectly by threatening to kill Pentagon or service budget requests
or proposals for new weapons unless their constituencies benefit.
Moreover, the Department of Defense and the military services,
dependent on military committees for approval of their budgets
and programmatic proposals, will tend to place extra contracts in
committee members' constituencies. Scholars generally argue that
this cooperation produces defense budgets that are too high and
skews the allocation of defense contracts away from a distribution
that would most effectively provide for the national defense.

A partisan version of distributive theory suggests that areas represented by members of the majority party in Congress tend to
benefit (e.g., Levitt and Snyder 1995). All MCs are assumed to want
government contracts in their constituencies. But only majority

party MCs have a dependable source of majority voting support. Thus they are better able to get defense contracts for their constituencies than are minority party MCs. As a result, majority party members are rewarded electorally. The military services go along because they need the support of the majority party in Congress. Places that elect majority party members would be expected to benefit at the expense of those electing minority party members.

A third version of distributive theory stresses the importance of MC ideology. The theory here is that places represented by relatively more conservative (or hawkish) MCs would tend to play a larger role in and benefit more from military procurement policy making. Majorities of congressional Republicans and conservative Democrats, mostly from the South, have made up the Conservative Coalition (CC) in Congress since the 1930s. During the cold war, the CC was the backbone of a bipartisan consensus on foreign and defense policy. The theory that CC members benefit from defense spending argues that the DOD, recognizing its dependence on this group in Congress, rewards CC members for their past support and ensures their future support by directing military procurement expenditures to their constituencies. The key theoretical point here is that ideology provides the basis for stable congressional support for defense spending.

The fourth distributive theory is universalism. Universalism theory contends that because majority party MCs want to reduce the risk of getting punished if their party loses majority control, they adopt a norm of universalism that results in benefiting constituencies represented by members of oversized or even unanimous congressional coalitions (Weingast 1979). Intrapolicy universalism suggests that because many places have businesses and workforces that could benefit from defense contracts, military procurement expenditures will have widespread geographic distribution. Interpolicy universalism, or reciprocity (Weingast 1979), predicts that the geographic distribution of military procurement spending is linked to a larger logroll that spreads across other policy areas. Scholars adopting this view generally assert that such a logroll is structured along committee lines (e.g., Weingast and Marshall 1988).

The fifth popular view is that distributive politics is minimally, or not at all, involved in determining the allocation of defense expenditures. Instead, defense expenditures are said to be directed to those places with greater economic capacity and without regard for which legislative constituencies will benefit (e.g., Mayer 1991). For example, Goss writes:

> Decisions about weapons acquisition are closely related to matters that affect the perceptions of foreign governments—especially potential enemies. While it is immaterial to potential enemies whether the Texas airfield site is chosen over the California site (the same Air Force commands them both) it is important that our technological capabilities be viewed with the utmost respect. If the Defense Department determines that one contractor can do a better job than another, even at slightly higher cost, it is difficult for the committee member to recommend that the inferior job be done. While . . . congressmen try to help their districts to get defense contracts, their apparent lack of effectiveness is most likely rooted in their acceptance that they do not have the information to make the final judgements on these matters. It is all well and good to boost one's own district, but if it is true, as the Defense Department may claim, that the contractor in the other fellow's district makes a better missile, it is best to try again on another slice of the defense pie. (1972: 232).

Effectiveness

All five theories about Congress's role in defense contracting make assumptions about the *effectiveness* of the resulting geographic distribution of military procurement expenditures. "Effective" distribution of federal expenditures is defined as one in which expenditures are targeted to the right places. Of course, what the "right places" are depends on whether one views effectiveness from a national defense or congressional distributive politics point of view. From a national defense perspective, expenditures are distributed effectively if they go to places that are best able to transform military procurement dollars into the goods and services deemed necessary to provide for the national defense. Expenditures would be ineffectively distributed if they were not targeted at such places. The first four of the theories discussed above contend that allocations that respond to MCs' committee, party, or ideological positions in Congress are *ineffective* from a national security perspective. The first three theories assume that policy benefits are targeted at places represented by incumbent MCs on defense committees, in the majority party, or in the Conservative Coalition, so that those MCs can gain or maintain votes in their constituencies. The fourth theory, universalism, assumes that benefits are widely spread among constituencies regardless of their capacity to produce the goods and services required for the national defense. The fifth view assumes that military contracts are distributed *effectively* from a national security perspective precisely because the influence of congressional politics is minimized. Thus distributing military procurement awards with an eye toward electoral incentives of MCs, an assumption that drives the first four versions of distributive theory, is assumed to be incompatible with targeting military procurement funds to places for national defense purposes. Indeed, "[n]ot even the most ardent advocate of preparedness can favor a system that blinds rational choice, retains old programs beyond their usefulness, and selects new ones according to the accidents of political influence" (Russett 1970: 183).

From a congressional distributive politics perspective, effectiveness consists of bringing benefits to constituents who will in turn vote for the incumbent MC or, if the incumbent does not run for reelection, a member of the incumbent's political party. The literature presents two positions on how the *electoral effectiveness* of federal spending might look. The *symbolic politics* position holds that as long as military procurement expenditures are awarded to his or her constituency, the MC can take credit for producing them, regardless of whether they are warranted by the constituency's capacity for producing the desired military goods and services or whether they are economically beneficial to the constituency (e.g., Mayhew 1974). The *economic development* position holds that a federal program or programmatic expenditure is effective only if it actually improves the economic condition of the constituency. The idea here is that constituents are induced to support the incumbent if he or she contributes materially to their well-being. Both positions take a constituency rather than a national perspective on effectiveness. The symbolic position would focus on whether factors such as committee representation, partisanship, ideology, or universalism influence the targeting of military procurement awards. The economic development perspective would go one step further to examine the impact of military procurement expenditures on local economies.

To summarize, the effectiveness of the distributive politics of military procurement spending can be evaluated relative to providing for the national defense as well as relative to the electoral incentives of MCs, with the latter being divided into purely symbolic and actual economic development. While various aspects of these ideas have received some attention in the literature, there has been virtually no scholarship explicitly devoted to the question of the effectiveness of the distributive politics of military procurement spending. Some scholars have examined the economic impact of defense spending on state economic development. For example, students of state economic development have found that states that receive higher levels of defense spending experience economic benefits from it (e.g, Brace 1993; Hansen 1993). Russett (1970) concedes this point in his argument that the way military procurement awards are distributed results in greater income inequality across states. However, the role played by distributive politics in shaping this effect has not been explored. The evidence is mixed regarding the economic impact of defense spending at the national level (Sandler and Hartley 1995), although most agree with Russett (1970) that defense spending has a negative impact on national economic growth. However, here too the extent to which distributive politics in Congress produces this negative effect on national economic growth remains unexamined. The dominant view in the congressional politics literature is that the electoral incentives of MCs are incompatible with any sort of policy effectiveness goals. Effective policy can be made only when the influence of congressional politics is muted. While often assumed, this view has itself rarely been analyzed. As a result, little attention has been given to examining the degree to which the goals of policy effectiveness and electoral effectiveness may be compatible. For example, if we assume that, all things being equal, voters would prefer expenditures targeted to deal with real policy problems over purely symbolic pork barrel spending, then the goals of policy effectiveness and electoral effectiveness may coincide (Wittman 1995).

The question of effectiveness can be considered both in terms of where policy expenditures are distributed—whether they are going to the "right" places—and in terms of the impact those expenditures have. Effectiveness can also be examined in terms of policy effectiveness or electoral effectiveness. Effectiveness must also be considered at both the national and subnational levels. The study of the distributive politics of military procurement that we present here cannot address all these aspects of effectiveness, but we do consider many of them. For example, targeting military procurement expenditures to those places best able to produce the goods and services needed for the national defense would be consistent with a nationally effective defense policy.[6] In terms of electoral effectiveness, each of the four distributive theories outlined above makes clear predictions about which constituencies would receive a disproportionate share of military procurement expenditures.[7] Regarding the resultant economic impact of military procurement, a nationally effective distribution of expenditures would be one that maximized aggregate national wealth. Similarly, it would be locally effective if it resulted in local economic growth.

We cannot present a comprehensive evaluation of the effectiveness of military procurement spending in this study. However, we examine several hypotheses related to effectiveness so as to consider whether distributive politics contributes to the effectiveness or ineffectiveness of military procurement policy.

PREVIOUS RESEARCH METHODOLOGIES

The anomaly that is the focus of this book—military procurement policy has the defining characteristics of distributive politics, but empirical research suggests it is not a distributive policy—stems primarily from the limited theoretical and empirical scope of previous research. Most studies have been snapshots of the geographic distribution of defense expenditures or defense employment at one point in time. They have not considered the enormous amount of intertemporal inertia in defense contracting and the fact that most distributive theories make predictions about *changes* in the targeting of benefits rather than the overall *level* of expenditures in localities. Moreover, most studies have not taken into account the possible reciprocal relationships that exist among defense procurement spending, congressional defense committee representation, and state economic conditions. Finally, most studies test only one of the various versions of distributive politics. These limitations are important to recognize, because what appear to be anomalous or conflicting interpretations may actually be compatible. Compatibility could occur in either (or both) of two ways: all or some of the processes implied in the alternative distributive politics explanations may work together at the same time, or different distributive politics processes may operate at different points in time.

ROAD MAP

The problem we have described thus far is that different kinds of distributive politics in Congress may (or may not) influence the geographic distribution of military procurement expenditures and defense committee representation, that where such expenditures go may (or may not) affect local economic conditions, and that the various types of distributive politics may contribute to or detract from the national defense and economic impacts of military procurement spending.

As this brief overview indicates, the literature on distributive politics has yet to settle on a fundamental model of that process, instead producing several apparently competing theories. Based on our critique of previous studies, we build an analytic model that we believe helps clarify our understanding of distributive politics. We extend the theoretical discussion to include the question of the effectiveness of distributive politics. We test the analytic model on a pooled cross section of year-to-year U.S. military procurement expenditure data covering the 1963–95 period. We also explore how the findings of the model change during this period. Based on this evidence, we draw conclusions about the nature and effectiveness of the distributive politics of military procurement spending.

In chapter 2 we present in more detail the several competing theories of distributive politics introduced here. We begin with how committees, parties, and ideology might influence the distribution of military procurement benefits. Following this discussion, we consider intrapolicy and interpolicy variants of the distributive theory known as universalism along with the claim made by some scholars that distributive politics is not operative in military procurement policy. We conclude our theoretical discussion by exploring the largely unexamined question of how effective the allocation of policy benefits can be.

In chapter 3 we focus our attention more specifically on the literature on military procurement spending. We evaluate the evidence regarding each of the distributive theories, paying particular attention to the limitations of current research. The literature shows a mixed bag of often-conflicting theories, research designs, and empirical findings.

In chapter 4 we develop an analytic model that is sufficiently broad in scope to allow us to evaluate predictions made by each of the distributive theories considered in chapter 2. A number of methodological issues are raised here, some of which are left to Appendix A. After presenting the analytic model, we describe several specific hypotheses and our research design.

Chapters 5 through 8 present findings from our analysis of the distributive politics of military procurement spending. Chapter 5 concentrates on the factors that influence year-to-year changes in the geographic distribution of military procurement expenditures. We find several factors working together, supporting the conclusion that a hybrid model of distributive politics is at work.

Chapter 6 explores the factors that influence changes in the probability that states are represented on defense committees in Congress. Separate analyses are presented for the House and the Senate. The findings support a hybrid model of defense committee representation. We also devote attention to how factors that directly influence defense committee representation may, as a result, indirectly affect the distribution of procurement awards based on our findings from chapter 5.

In chapter 7 we use the findings reported in chapters 5 and 6 to estimate the over-time accumulation of the effects that various factors in our analytic model have on both the distribution of benefits and committee representation. We show how the year-to-year changes in procurement expenditures at the margin lead to substantial changes over longer periods. Chapter 7 also includes a discussion of the overall fit of our analytic model, paying particular attention to how well our analysis of the 1963 to 1995 period accounts for the observed geographic distribution of military procurement expenditures and defense committee representation in 1995, the final year included in our analysis.

Chapter 8 takes our examination of the dynamics of distributive politics one step further. We conduct a series of analyses on successive five-year increments of our data to explore whether and how the factors that influence the distribution of military procurement awards and defense committee representation change over time. This chapter is anchored by a discussion of several competing theories about when one should expect to observe different types and degrees of distributive politics effects in military procurement spending.

Chapter 9 shifts from the distributive politics of military procurement to an analysis of the resulting impact of military procurement spending. We consider both the national defense and the economic development effects of such spending and what portion of that impact can be attributed to distributive politics.

In the last chapter we present our conclusions. We argue that military procurement spending is not an anomaly vis-à-vis distributive politics theories of legislative policy making but that the distributive politics of this policy is different from what has previously been conjectured. We summarize a hybrid theory of distributive politics and discuss its implications for understanding congressional policy making more generally.

CHAPTER TWO

The Distributive Politics of Military Procurement Spending

Various types of distributive politics, according to different views held by political scientists, may or may not characterize military procurement policy. Here we describe the logic and implications of committee, party, ideology, universalism, and "no effect" theories of distributive politics. Each is considered in isolation to facilitate drawing out its particular implications. However, elements of more than one of these theories may work together as parts of the distributive politics of defense procurement. Our analysis is designed to explore the extent to which they do.

THEORETICAL BACKGROUND

Distributive theories of politics focus on how the reelection goals of members of Congress combine with the organizational structure of legislative policy making to affect the geographic distribution of policy benefits. Lowi's (1964) definition of distributive politics argues that a particular type of policy generates a particular type of politics, in some ways mixing outcomes and process into a single definition. Wilson (1973) develops a typology of policies based on whether the benefits of a policy and the resulting costs are distributed broadly or narrowly. In doing so, he makes a clear distinction between process and outcomes, with his definition of a policy as distributive focused on outcomes. Rundquist and Fere-john (1975) and Arnold (1979) instead define distributive politics in terms of the process of legislative targeting of policy benefits. We adopt a definition of distributive theory that focuses primarily on processes of benefit targeting and committee representation, although we return to the question of defining distributive politics in our concluding chapter.

Distributive theories generate predictions about the character-istics of the policy-making process that influence *change* in the geo-graphic distribution of benefits. Thus distributive theories explic-itly view policy making as dynamic: the geographic distribution of policy benefits at any one time represents the unfolding of a dynamic process of decision making that preceded it.

Distributive theories begin with the assumption that MCs are primarily concerned with their own reelection (Mayhew 1974) and behave and enact policy so as to achieve this goal.[1] As we will see, different versions of distributive theory describe different concep-tions of the policy-making process in Congress and how congres-sional policy making relates to the policy outputs of the government. Distributive theories generate predictions about the geographic distribution of policy benefits, but we do not define whether a pol-icy is distributive based on that resulting distribution. Distributive theories describe the political processes that produce the resulting geographic distribution of benefits more than they describe the level of concentration or dispersion of benefits. That is why through-out this book we talk about distributive politics rather than dis-tributive policies.

The theories considered here may be thought of as alternative answers to the question, how does a legislature organize itself so as to solve the collective action problems associated with policy making to produce decisions that meet the needs of its members? In fact, Krehbiel (1991: 247) asserts that distributive theories depict "a legislature as a collective choice body whose principal task is to allocate policy benefits."[2] The committee, party, and ideology the-ories of distributive politics each focus on an institutional structure or decision-making rule that allows legislators to solve collective action problems in a manner that allows something less than a universalistic winning coalition to be formed and maintained. For example, Aldrich (1995: 34–35) argues that legislators create parties to reduce the transaction costs involved in policy making, thereby providing more stability to the policy-making process. Similarly, the committee theory suggests that gains from exchange allow even minority voting coalitions (committee members) to reap policy benefits via logrolling even if true preferences reveal that a majority of chamber members opposed specific policies. Both parties and committees are assumed to be able to solve collective action problems and produce legislative decisions because they reduce the uncertainty associated with forming and maintaining a governing coalition. Similarly, ideological theory applied to the U.S. Congress would argue that the so-called Conservative Coalition of Republicans and conservative (often southern) Democrats provides the same sort of stability and certainty in the politics of military spending that others argue is provided by parties or committees. To use the jargon, committees, political parties, or ideology can serve as Shepsle's (1979) "structures" that can produce an equilibrium in collective decision making among lawmakers.

Given this perspective, universalism can be viewed as arguing that none of these institutional or decision-rule arrangements successfully overcomes the collective action problems that reelection-oriented policy makers face with sufficient certainty to prevent a less-than-universal coalition from coming unwound.[3] Universalism is a solution to the collective action problem in that it provides a means by which policy decisions can be made, but it implies that the benefits of a policy will be distributed more widely than the committee, party, or ideology theories would predict. Universalism emerges from the assumption that while any one minimum winning coalition would produce greater benefits to the winning coalition members, uncertainty exists regarding who will be members of the coalition (Weingast 1979; Shepsle and Weingast 1981; Niou and Ordeshook 1985). Faced with this uncertainty, MCs opt for legislation that distributes benefits to all or nearly all members. This represents a failure in the sense that the net payoff per MC will be lower under universalism than would be the case under the other three versions of distributive theory.

COMMITTEE

Committee-centered theories of distributive politics occupy a central position in political scientists' accounts of public policy formation in Congress. These theories contend that reelection-oriented MCs representing diverse constituencies seek membership on committees that allow them to obtain

> a favorable distribution of pork barrel projects, expenditures targeted to their districts, and policy outcomes desired by favored constituents. Since the environment for obtaining favorable distributions of these things is highly competitive, members need to make deals, form alliances, and engage in vote trading and log rolling in order to succeed; in short, members need to cooperate. (Shepsle and Weingast, 1995: 7–8).

Committees grant "gains from trade" to their members. According to Shepsle and Weingast (1995: 10), a gain from trade occurs when "the value a legislator places on his or her own project . . . exceeds the burden he or she must bear in supporting the projects of other legislators."

In other words, Congress creates the committee system to generate cooperation so that each MC can realize gains from exchange and thereby meet the demands of his or her constituents. Committees are given jurisdiction over policy areas, not just specific pork barrel projects, which facilitates maintaining the long-term stability of the legislative process. Institutionalizing the solution in this manner reduces the costs associated with making a series of deals among individual MCs to pass every policy. If committees also have jurisdiction over subsequent proposals made by noncommittee members to change earlier decisions supported by the committee, committee members can keep deals from being reneged on, from unraveling as a result of unforeseen events, or from becoming too expensive once they reach the floor (Shepsle and Weingast 1995: 11). The long-term result is logrolling among committees, which results in benefits being directed disproportionately to constituencies represented by their MCs on committees with jurisdiction over particular policy areas (e.g., Weingast and Marshall 1988).

Krehbiel (1991) adds another dimension to the rationale for creating a formal committee structure in Congress. He focuses on the consequences of uncertainty regarding the outcomes that may result if particular policy alternatives are adopted. Reducing uncertainty about how policy alternatives will affect MCs' interests is just as much a collective action problem for members of Congress as is facilitating gains from exchange. A committee system structured around substantive policy areas provides an institutional solution to this collective need for policy-specific expertise by encouraging committee members to develop such expertise. The implications for the composition of committees in Krehbiel's informational model are different from those in the straight committee-centered distributive theory. Krehbiel's informational theory predicts that committee membership will more accurately reflect the distribution of policy preferences of noncommittee members in a legislative chamber, whereas the committee- centered distributive theory predicts that committees will be composed of members whose policy preferences are distinctly different from those of others in the chamber. However, both views share the more general assumption that the committee system addresses the collective action problems that face reelection-oriented members of Congress.

A number of specific hypotheses are implied by the committee-based distributive theory. On the supply side, one of these is the benefit hypothesis (e.g., Arnold 1979), which predicts that constituencies represented on any given committee tend to have their interests better served (i.e., benefited) by policies under the committee's jurisdiction than do nonmembers' constituencies. This may be because committee members proactively direct benefits back to their constituents in an effort to win votes in the next election. Or it may be because budget-constrained bureaucrats see to it that committee members' districts benefit so that committee members have an incentive to support their budget requests. As Arnold argues, defense committee members are in a better position (than nonmembers) to bargain with the bureaucracy,

> for they control a wide range of services needed by Pentagon officials. These are discretionary services that committee members may provide or withhold as they please. . . . One of the most important services . . . is to lead coalitions for whatever causes they seek to advance in Congress, whether budgets, weapons systems, pay, or benefits. (1979: 98)

In addition, the committee-centered distributive theory suggests that the relationship between constituency interest and legislative policy making also exists on the input or demand side. Accordingly, the committee recruitment hypothesis suggests that reelection-seeking MCs from constituencies with a certain kind of interest seek and obtain membership on committees that deal with policies concerning that interest or, in other words, that the committee assignment process will be governed by self-selection (Krehbiel 1991: 43). Thus MCs from constituencies with economic interests in defense contracting will seek and acquire membership on relevant committees to promote and protect that interest. In Arnold's (1979) interpretation, bureaucrats create both the outcome predicted in the benefit hypothesis and much of the constituency pressure implied in the recruitment hypothesis. Thus,

> by favoring the members' constituencies when they make allocation decisions . . . [bureaucrats] give congressmen publicity, a healthy local economy, and the opportunity for credit claiming. . . . It [also] means that a large proportion of his constituents will be military employees and, thus, directly interested in certain defense issues. . . . Local benefits also help restrain committee members from leading coalitions *against*

projects advocated by Pentagon officials. (Arnold 1979: 98–99; original emphasis).

By extension, if being on a committee benefits MCs and their constituencies, the committee-based theory implies that an area represented on a committee would be likely to *retain* that representation because the member would have less incentive to transfer to another committee than if his or her district did not benefit. We refer to this hypothesis as the committee-centered retention hypothesis.

Related to both the recruitment and retention hypotheses is the over-representation (Rundquist and Ferejohn 1975) or committee-outlier hypothesis (e.g., Krehbiel 1991: 43). To facilitate gains from trade, congressional committees must be composed of representatives who come from congressional districts with higher demand for the policy benefits that each committee controls (e.g., Adler and Lapinski 1997: 895) than do noncommittee members' constituencies. Of course, Krehbiel's information theory suggests the opposite hypothesis: that all committees will represent the distribution of preferences in their parent chamber.

As generally presented, the committee version of distributive theory assumes that the resulting distribution of policy benefits will not be effective. Instead of policy expenditures being directed to places that are best able to use those funds to produce the desired public outcome or to places with the greatest relative need for such expenditures, the committee-based distributive theory predicts that funds will go disproportionately to places represented by MCs on the relevant congressional committees, regardless of their capacity or need.

PARTY

Aldrich (1995) and Cox and McCubbins (1993) argue that political parties are the intentional creations of political elites in response to the pressure to create long-term solutions to a series of collective action problems that all democratic governments face. Political

parties help to produce order and stability in what would otherwise be a chaotic environment where voting majorities both in the
electorate and in Congress would be highly volatile. While at least
partially endogenous to the political process—they are created and
re-created by political elites—political parties serve as institutions
that allow for more predictability in democratic politics.

Aldrich (1995: 29–36) argues that the incentives of legislators
dealing with distributive policies reinforce the attraction of creating
political parties. He shows that a variety of sets of policy preferences
among legislators may lead to a collective action problem and that
such preferences need not be associated with what are tradition-
ally described as distributive policies (p. 39).[4] Aldrich concludes
that a subset (though at least a majority) of members of a legislature can benefit over the long term if they can reach a binding agreement to cooperate, and political parties are the institutions they
create to foster and enforce such cooperation. In the extreme, parties reduce the number of possible minimum winning coalitions to
one (members of the majority party), which eliminates the need for
broader, or universal, coalitions to pass legislation (Weingast 1979;
Shepsle and Weingast 1981; Niou and Ordeshook 1985).

Thus parties are created because they serve the interests of individual members of Congress. However, once a party is created and
MCs become identified with it, individual MCs develop an incentive to serve, at least partially, the interests of the party as a collective entity. Cox and McCubbins (1993) argue that the reputation of
the party becomes an electoral resource for candidates from that
party. Party labels serve as information cues, or "brand names,"
that efficiently convey to voters large amounts of information about
candidates. Thus MCs have an interest in avoiding behavior (votes
or otherwise) that detracts from their party's reputation. This results
in a symbiotic, or endogenous, relationship between the party as
a collective and MCs as individuals serving their own and each
other's needs. Of course, protecting the reputation of a political
party is also a collective action problem. Yet Cox and McCubbins
(1993: 109–17) provide evidence that the collective fates of con-

gressional candidates are tied together through partisanship, and parties do retain some ability to punish MCs who do not toe the party line. Similarly, Cain, Ferejohn, and Fiorina (1987) describe the importance of party labels in voters' decisions to support incumbents as well as in facilitating policy congruence between MCs and their constituents as MCs work to develop the "personal vote."[5] Combined, these factors appear to provide sufficient rationale for and evidence of party maintenance voting behavior among MCs.

Cox and McCubbins (1993) maintain that the majority party is the dominant institution organizing policy making in Congress. Majority party leaders realize that they can continue to lead the majority party only as long as more members of their party than of the opposition party are reelected. Because the majority party typically elects the parliamentary leader (e.g., the Speaker of the House) and appoints new members to standing committees, it can influence the organization of the committee system so as to facilitate their members' reelection. In this view, the committee system is merely an institutional tool used by the majority party to maintain the long-term benefits resulting from cooperation among party members. By deferring to members' preferences for committee assignments, party leaders can give them control over the type of programs of most concern to their constituents. This allows majority party MCs to pursue their reelection interests, which simultaneously serves the party's interest in maintaining its majority status. Because parties drive the process, any intercommittee logrolling that takes place may be between majority party members on different committees—that is, *within* the majority party. This view of distributive politics implies that defense benefits will be found to favor the constituencies of majority party members (the pure majority party benefit hypothesis), or at least those majority party members on the defense committees.

The party theory also suggests that majority party members will have more incentive to join a committee with jurisdiction over large amounts of discretionary spending than do minority party members, because majority party members can expect to benefit more from committee representation (the majority party committee recruitment hypothesis). Similarly, areas represented on committees by members of the majority party should be better able to retain their seats (the majority party committee retention hypothesis). Accordingly, assuming that majority party leaders are accommodationist regarding party members' committee requests, the majority side of constituency-serving committees should be found to overrepresent constituencies with a high demand for programs under the committees' jurisdiction (the majority party committee overrepresentation hypothesis). Because majority party members of constituency-serving committees are better able to benefit their constituencies, they should be more likely than minority party members to be reelected (the majority party reelection hypothesis).

The party theory also implies that in the short run the impact of party-centered distributive politics will make both the national defense and the economy at least as ineffective as does committee-centered distributive politics. This is because places capable of efficiently producing for the military will not receive procurement contracts if they are represented by minority party members.

To summarize, the party-based distributive theory suggests that the processes described by the committee-centered theory may operate, but if they do, they operate within the confines of the majority party. The resulting implications for the effectiveness of distributive politics are similar to those for the committee-based theory. Thus the goal of maintaining majority party status, a political goal, is assumed to be at odds with producing effective public policy. Rather than target places with the capacity to produce the desired goods and services for the national defense or having the desired impact on local economic development, the party-based view anticipates that committee representation and benefits will be given to places represented by majority party MCs.

IDEOLOGY

Ideology has been defined as a coherent worldview or integrated set of policy positions (e.g. Downs 1957; Hinich and Munger 1994).

Ideology may lead MCs to join certain committees, pursue certain policy objectives, and vote for and against various policy alternatives, regardless of whether their constituencies benefit materially. Shared ideologies may bring MCs together to form a stable, if less formal, voting coalition. Poole and Rosenthal (1997) argue that much of the past one hundred fifty years of congressional roll call voting can be understood as being structured by a single ideological dimension, interrupted occasionally by periods when a second dimension emerges. Finding such a simple ideological structure in roll call voting behavior contrasts with the expectation of instability in democratic decision making predicted by many spatial theories of voting (for a review, see Mueller 1989). Poole and Rosenthal's (1997) finding of limited dimensionality in the ideological space of Congress also fits well with Hinich and Munger's conclusion that ideology in the mass public exhibits a simple (one- or two-) dimensional structure. Thus ideology can be seen as providing a solution to the collective action problems that legislatures face in a manner similar to the argument Aldrich (1995) makes regarding political parties.

Both arguments have roots in Arrow's (1951) and Black's (1958) discoveries that single-dimensional collective decision making yields stable and predictable outcomes. However, separating ideology from other factors has proven to be difficult. Both Poole and Rosenthal (1997) and Hinich and Munger (1994) find that the limited ideological dimensionality they observe is structured along party lines. This makes sense given that as parties organize they do so at least in part around shared policy goals. However, these findings beg the question of whether partisanship and ideology are possibly independent influences on the policy-making behavior of MCs. Of relevance to distributive theory, separating MC ideology from constituency interest has also proven difficult (Jackson and Kingdon 1992).

Despite the difficulty in parsing out its unique role, several scholars have argued that ideology is significant for explaining legislative behavior regarding defense policy (e.g., Moyer 1973; Lindsay

1991). The classic example of this in the U.S. context is the Conservative Coalition of Republicans and conservative (often southern) Democrats that has emerged periodically in Congress. Ideology as it relates to defense spending usually denotes an MC's "hawkishness" as opposed to "dovishness." As it concerns distributive politics, ideology is usually seen as a cause of behavior that competes with the motivation to obtain parochial material benefits of concern to a constituency (e.g., Lindsay 1991). In the defense context, the implication is that hawks are more likely than doves to join defense committees, defense committees will tend to be ideological outliers (i.e., more hawkish) relative to their parent chambers, and Congress's defense decisions will tend to be hawkish. As Mayer (1991: 10) puts it, "[T]he decision to continue production [of a weapons system] or end it is usually more a matter of strategy and ideology than jobs or pork."

Some analysts, however, note that ideology-based and interest-based motivations are difficult to disentangle operationally (Lindsay 1991; Jackson and Kingdon 1992). MCs who are hawks may be more likely to come from constituencies with strong preferences (ideological or material) for increased defense spending. The question is whether MCs seek membership on defense committees because of their ideologies or because their constituencies are economically dependent on defense spending. Voting hawkishly on a weapons system may simply reflect an MC's constituency's interest (Lindsay 1991). If so, then there is no ideology-based benefit hypothesis separate from constituency interest. However, if an ideological effect can be uncovered that is independent of constituency interest, an ideology-based benefit hypothesis emerges.

The straight-forward ideology benefit hypothesis is that places represented in Congress by conservatives or hawks will receive disproportionately greater benefits from defense spending (the pure ideology benefit hypothesis). This may result from the military services and the Department of Defense rewarding conservative MCs for their support of defense spending and punishing liberal MCs for their opposition. Of course, it may also be that such ideological effects are conditioned by representation on defense committees such that only states represented by conservatives on defense committees benefit (the conditional ideology/committee benefit hypothesis). For example, Dering (1998) finds that military bases located in districts represented on defense committees by liberals were more likely to be targeted for closure during the 1980s and 1990s.[6]

The ideology theory suggests that committee recruitment favors members with a certain ideological orientation rather than certain constituency interests (the ideological recruitment hypothesis). In the case of defense committees, the tendency is to recruit more hawkish or conservative members. If committee membership helps MCs to obtain their ideological policy goals, conservative members will tend to be retained on the committees (the ideological retention hypothesis). If a member's constituents tend to be conservative and if membership on a defense committee is viewed by constituents as evidence of a member's conservatism, then conservative committee members should be more likely to be reelected (the ideological reelection hypothesis). As a result of their tendency to attract and retain conservative members, the defense committees will tend to overrepresent ideologically conservative members relative to their parent chambers (the ideological over-representation/outlier hypothesis).

The same sorts of expectations regarding policy effectiveness that we have described under the committee and party distributive theories apply to the ideology theory as well. Committee representation and the targeting of benefits on the basis of MC ideology are assumed to be inconsistent with what would constitute an effective distribution of military procurement awards.

To explore and clarify each view, we have presented the committee, party, and ideology theories of distributive politics largely in isolation of each other. In the process, however, we may have created the impression that we expect distributive politics to be characterized by one of these three ideals. That is not the case. A more realistic expectation is that the distributive politics of military procurement spending may evidence elements of all three theories. The question may be one of relative importance among the three theories rather than of choosing one approach to the exclusion of the other two. Moreover, the three distributive processes may also interact with each other so as to influence policy making, or their relative importance may change over time. We explore all of these possibilities later, but for now we prefer the clarity afforded by separate discussions of each theoretical factor.

UNIVERSALISM

Mayhew (1974: 88) described universalism as the legislative situation in which "every member, regardless of party or seniority, has a right to his share of benefits." Underlying universalism, according to Fiorina (1977) and Weingast (1979), is each MC's uncertainty about being a member of the "minimum winning coalition" necessary to pass a bill. A minimum winning coalition is the coalition of MCs that constitutes the smallest number necessary to enact the proposed legislation.[7] MCs would benefit more by becoming members of a minimum winning coalition because benefits would only have to be divided among coalition members. However, being a member of the losing coalition would get them nothing at all. As a protection against the possibility of being excluded from the minimum winning coalition or from being dropped from what was a minimum winning coalition as coalition membership shifts, MCs might adopt the norm of universalism. Universalism guarantees that every MC gets something. In other words, reelection constrained, risk averse legislators opt for a sure something to take home to their constituencies rather than only the chance of being able to take home a larger part of the available policy benefits. Compared to our committee, party, and ideology theories of distributive politics, universalism suggests that each of these previous three institutional arrangements is unable to structure and maintain a governing coalition for any length of time. In its broadest sense universalism implies that committees, parties, and ideology do not solve the collective action problems associated with policy making.

Although first formulated in regard to policy making within committees, universalism can and has been expanded to explain the organization of whole legislatures (e.g., Fiorina 1981: 198; Weingast and Marshall 1988). Empirically, universalism predicts two different but theoretically linked phenomena: the allocation of distributive benefits to nearly every district by an omnibus bill and passage of these bills by lopsided majorities in committee and on the floor (Soherr-Hadwiger 1998: 59).

There are three variants of universalism that we can describe as they relate to military procurement spending. The first is a fairly naive view of what we call intrapolicy universalism. This view suggests that military contracts will be distributed to all or nearly all states roughly equally. Mayer (1991) and Lindsay (1991) apparently allude to this naive intrapolicy universalism in the military procurement case when they refer to the tendency of prime contractors to distribute subcontracts universalistically. However, most scholars reject the notion that benefits within any one policy area are likely to be equally spread out without regard to constituency demand for and interest in them. Figure 1.1 and the analysis presented in chapter 5 reject out of hand the idea that military procurement spending is equally distributed across states without regard to state-specific causal factors. Thus, while the naive view of intra-policy universalism exists as an ideal type, it lacks empirical support and serves as nothing more than a theoretical straw man.

A more sophisticated version of intrapolicy universalism suggests that within any single policy area states with an economic interest in receiving benefits will receive them. In the case of military procurement expenditures, places with an economic interest in obtaining such benefits will receive a disproportionate share of them. We have already noted the difficulty in separating a constituency's economic interest from an MC's ideology, although doing so is fundamental to evaluating universalism as a theory of distributive politics. As we return periodically to the discussion of intrapolicy universalism, our attention will be on this version of the theory rather than the naive version.

A third view of universalism would treat military procurement as one part of a grand multipolicy logroll. We label this version interpolicy universalism. Like the more sophisticated intrapolicy universalism, interpolicy universalism predicts that states with economic interests in military contracts will receive them. But in this case, it is accomplished through across-policy logrolling that is structured by committees.[8] Thus the economic interest in receiving military procurement contracts leads MCs to seek and acquire representation on congressional defense committees, which in turn results in military procurement expenditures being directed back to the constituencies of defense committee members.

The implications of universalism theory for what influences committee representation are less clear. Since intrapolicy universalism predicts that all MCs with an interest in defense procurement expenditures will benefit regardless of whether they are on defense committees, there is little incentive for MCs representing defense interests to seek seats on these committees. Thus the reelection pressures that drive committee representation in the party- and committee-based distributive theories will not produce this behavior in intrapolicy universalism theory. A possible secondary implication is that with everyone capable of obtaining military procurement benefits, intrapolicy universalism allows for committee representation to be determined by other factors, such as ideology or special expertise in defense policy.

Interpolicy universalism, on the other hand, implies that MCs who want military procurement contracts tend to join defense committees and as a result are able to benefit their constituencies. The interpolicy version of universalism, similar to that developed by Weingast and Marshall (1988), suggests that both committee representation and committee vetoes of proposals that would change the distribution of military procurement benefits ensure the stability of interpolicy logrolling. This theory yields the same prediction made by the committee-centered distributive theory: places represented by committee members will benefit.

Much has been written about the presumed inefficiencies of universalism (Weingast, Shepsle, and Johnson 1981; Niou and Ordeshook 1985; Weingast and Marshall 1988). Since universalism presumes that members from constituencies with an economic interest in receiving military procurement expenditures will either get them (intrapolicy universalism) or seek and obtain defense committee representation and participate in across-policy logrolls to get them (interpolicy universalism), the key to determining the effectiveness of universalism is in defining what constitutes a constituency's "economic interest." If "economic interest" in receiving military procurement expenditures stems from an existing capacity to translate them into the desired military goods or from a need for economic development, universalism should be viewed as effectively targeting military procurement benefits. On the other hand, if a constituency's "economic interest" stems from previous economic dependence on military contracting or noneconomic factors such as constituency or MC ideology, the effectiveness of universalism is more questionable.[9]

NO DISTRIBUTIVE EFFECTS
(OR EFFECTIVE BENEFIT DISTRIBUTION?)

Arguments for why there is no distributive politics of military procurement spending are forcefully made by several political scientists. For example, Mayer (1991: 3) argues that it is a myth that "Congress supports major weapons systems because defense contracts produce jobs in many congressional districts and states [and that] [i]t will not cancel weapons because doing so sacrifices economic benefits." He concludes that "the Pentagon does not, indeed can not, distribute defense contracts (as opposed to bases) for political purposes" (p. 210).

Further political explanations of contracting decisions

describe neither process nor outcome adequately and over-
simplify a vastly complicated decision-making structure.
Indeed, one reason pork barrel explanations are so attractive
is that they are simple, parsimonious, and persuasive. They
are also mostly wrong. (Mayer 1991: 210)

While Mayer acknowledges that partisanship and ideology play
a role in defense procurement policy, he argues that the nature of
the procurement process itself precludes any effect of congressional politics on the actual distribution of military procurement
expenditures:

At the early stages in the acquisition cycle, then, responsibil-
ity is too fragmented and dispersed to permit political con-
tamination. At the later stages, most decisions have been set
in stone. Neither phase is amenable to congressional med-
dling. . . . The reason that people believe that politics drives
defense contracting is that most players in the process, especially those in Congress, pretend that it does, fostering the
impression is a useful electoral tool (1991: 139, 142).

Goss (1972) also argues that although distributive politics may
affect the geographic distribution of some kinds of defense expenditures, for example, expenditures for employment and military
bases, it cannot affect the distribution of military procurement
spending because MCs defer to military experts who say that particular weapons are necessary for strategic defense reasons. Goss
quotes Peck and Scherer's (1962) influential conclusion:

In general, we would conclude that political considerations
have not played a really major role in the choice of contractors for advanced weapons programs. Our research disclosed
no instances in which firms were selected for which a non-
political justification could not be made—always there were
at least some long-run considerations arguing for their choice.
It is reasonable to conclude from the available evidence that

political influences seldom lead to decisions which are seriously uneconomic from both short-run and long-run points
of view.

This conclusion will be greeted with skepticism by many
veterans of the weapons industry. It could be that we have
not penetrated sufficiently into the establishment to see fully
the political influences at work. It is also possible that partic-
ipants in the weapons business have been misled as to the
importance of political influence. Clearly, considerable political activity accompanies the selection of contractors. One
might well conclude that so much effort must have a corre-
sponding effect.

But much of this political activity has a ritualistic flavor. A
congressman will inquire about a selection action at the
request of an influential constituent, even when he doubts
that it will make any difference. The service responds to the
congressional inquiry with cordiality, but such inquiries may
have little impact at the operating levels where the source
selection decision is usually made. . . . [M]any of the political
pressures cancel out. . . . In any event we can only report what
we have seen; that politics counts for less in selecting weapons
contractors than many people think. (Goss 1972: 227)

The implication of the arguments made by Goss, Mayer, Peck
and Scherer, and others is that the subnational distribution of
defense procurement contracts is driven by the capacity of places
to produce the goods and services needed to provide for the national
defense. Mayer and Goss seem to be saying that military procurement dollars tend to be effectively targeted.

Taking a somewhat different view of the feasibility of distributive politics to influence the distribution of defense procurement
benefits, Cox and McCubbins (1993) argue that even if the defense
committees overrepresent constituencies involved in defense contracting, this will not result in more benefits for these constituencies

because most nondefense committees in the House are not interest outliers relative to their parent chambers in their policy areas.

> [A] handful of committees are dominated by preference out-liers and can be expected to draft legislation that, not being reflective of broader House interests, requires reciprocity among House committees to be passed. . . . [But] reciprocity would not be forthcoming from the vast majority of House committees since they have no need for inter-committee logrolls and would therefore only bear the costs of passing leg-islation that did not reflect their interests. (Cox and McCub-bins,: 79–82).

So, if distributive politics requires vote trading across committees, as in interpolicy universalism, Cox and McCubbins argue that MCs on defense committees would have no one with whom to trade.

If there is no potential electoral payoff in allocating defense con-tracts to particular places, then the principal assumption underly-ing the various versions of distributive theory is absent (see Mayer 1991: 53). The expectation is that defense procurement contracts will be awarded based on the ability to produce military goods and services and not based on committee, party, ideological, or uni-versalistic considerations. If this is true, the question of who gets appointed to defense committees is moot.

DOES DISTRIBUTIVE POLITICS PRODUCE AN EFFECTIVE BENEFIT DISTRIBUTION?

The assumed outcomes of the various distributive theories of mil-itary procurement spending concern their expected electoral, pol-icy, and economic impacts. The electoral connection is widely assumed and more often studied than the policy and economic impacts. Although our modeling and empirical testing focuses on the policy and economic impact of the distributive politics of defense procurement spending, we discuss all three here.

Electoral Impact

We have noted that distributive theories of politics assume that directing increased benefits back to a constituency will increase the reelection chances of the incumbent whose constituency benefits. For example, the committee-centered reelection hypothesis is that by delivering constituency services via their committee membership, incumbents will be viewed more favorably by constituents. Incumbents will acquire a "personal vote" from people who support them, not because they are members of the incumbent's political party or because they share the incumbent's policy orientation, but because they view the incumbent as someone who has benefited the constituency (e.g., Cain, Ferejohn, and Fiorina 1987). Arnold (1990) refers to this as voting by means of the incumbent performance rule. This personal vote will provide a margin that in most cases will result in the incumbent's reelection. Most studies of the electoral impact of federal spending have been fairly inconclusive (e.g., Feldman and Jondrow 1984), but Stein and Bickers (1994) report evidence of a conditional relationship and Cain, Ferejohn, and Fiorina (1987) suggest such a relationship between an incumbent's project work and voters' candidate evaluations. Alternative reelection-based distributive theories, such as the party version explored by Levitt and Snyder (1995), are also inconclusive. But Levitt and Snyder (1997) report that federal spending benefits congressional incumbents electorally. Schmit (2000) finds that parts of congressional districts that benefit from military procurement spending tend to provide more votes for incumbents in subsequent elections. She also reports that places that provide the most votes are subsequently rewarded with the most military contracts.

National Security Impact

Distributive theories generally assume that the resulting distribution of policy benefits will be ineffective in providing for whatever national need serves as the rationale for the policy (e.g., Cain,

Ferejohn, and Fiorina 1987). In regard to military procurement spending, biasing its distribution so as to benefit, for example, committee members' states is presumed to be an ineffective way to obtain weapons needed to meet national defense needs. As Russett put it:

> [W]e must not forget that a failure of deterrence can also come from a neglect of our weapons, both current and projected. Until there is an essential change in the international system, a failure to buy a needed new weapon could have effects just as calamitous as a runaway arms race. The country needs a mixture of carefully chosen weapons, both conventional and nuclear, to meet a variety of possible threats. (1970: 183)

National Economic Impact

Sandler and Hartley (1995) report that evidence regarding the impact of the level of defense spending on a nation's economy is mixed, but they conclude that it generally results in reducing national economic growth. Russett (1970) also argues that the distributive politics of military procurement spending results in decreasing economic growth nationally and that it increases income inequality, both nationally and regionally. Most large nonmilitary federal programs, at least until the 1980s, were aimed at or at least justified in terms of their impact on the poor and on developing local economies. Defense spending, especially that for military procurement, was presumed not to do this. Rather,

> the relatively high income regions—the Far West and the Northeast—usually receive shares of defense work that are above their shares of the national income. Similarly, the medium- or average-income regions—the Great Lakes, Plains, and Rocky Mountain states—receive shares of defense work that are below their national income shares. For the Southeast and Southwest there is some ambiguity. According to some

estimates these lowest-income states also receive less than their income share of defense work; . . . many of them now get slightly more, which indicates a mild tendency toward the reduction of income inequality at the lower extremity. Overall, however, there is an income redistribution effect in favor of the rich states.

[O]f all major federal expenditure programs, only DOD and NASA spending had this regressive effect—but . . . the regressiveness was strong enough to wipe out the progressive income redistribution of all other federal programs. Other studies show that even within industry and employment groups, defense spending makes the rich richer. The reason is the need in most weapons manufacture for a highly skilled and therefore expensive labor force. (Russett 1970: 130)

Russett (1970: 129) concludes that, "[n]ot only does defense procurement benefit some regions more than others, it has a regressive effect on the nation's income structure." The result is that rather than help to meet the needs of economically disadvantaged areas in the country, the distribution of defense spending helps the rich get richer. One could add, however, that while this distribution might be regressive in nature, if it creates a larger boost to GNP than would result if benefits were directed to relatively less well-off places, then the resulting impact could be argued to be economically effective from a national perspective.

Theories of distributive politics generally presume that the resulting distribution of military procurement spending interferes with the effective provision of national defense and decreases national economic growth because benefits are allocated to places with political clout rather than to places with the most capacity to produce the most bang for the buck. The classic public good interpretation is that defense spending by itself interferes with economic growth by allocating societal resources to the production of goods and services for which there is little private sector demand. Distributive politics is thought to contribute to this national effect.

In contrast, starting from the same reelection-oriented assumption about MCs, one can argue that the distributive politics of defense spending will produce an effective national distribution of expenditures. Such an argument begins with the assumption that reelection-oriented MCs have an incentive to try to solve their constituents' problems (Wittman 1995) rather than simply take symbolic positions on issues (e.g., Mayhew 1974) or deliver pork barrel expenditures to their constituencies regardless of their effectiveness (Niou and Ordeshook 1985). National problems exhibit subnational variation in their geographic distribution. We have noted that the capacity to produce the goods and services needed for national defense varies considerably across states. If military procurement benefits are directed to such high-capacity places and, more important, if distributive politics facilitates this tendency, then distributive politics can be said to promote the effective distribution of military contracts and the effective provision of the national defense.

Local Economic Impact

From the perspective of state economies, however, the picture changes. Brace (1993) shows that states that receive relatively higher levels of defense spending tend to experience higher levels of economic growth. Sandler and Hartley (1995) also report evidence suggesting that defense-related firms show higher profit margins than non-defense-related industries. Thus what Russett and others describe as economically counterproductive at the national level may produce positive economic benefits to at least some states.

From a local economic impact standpoint, a local problem may be the existence of a large segment of industry designed to provide goods and services for the military. If military contracts are not forthcoming, this capacity will go to waste and the local economy will suffer. Thus if military contracts go to such places, they can be said to be effectively targeted both from a national defense and from a local economic impact perspective. If one or more of the distributive theories we have described is associated with such areas getting contracts, distributive politics could be credited (at least in part) for the effective targeting of capacity.

Several scholars argue that military spending has a positive impact on local economies (e.g., Cain, Ferejohn, and Fiorina, 1987; Brace 1993). Local economic development may be only a secondary goal of military procurement spending from the Pentagon's point of view, but the local economic consequences of changes in defense spending must certainly be politically salient to MCs. To the extent that more defense contracts go to places with relatively greater need for economic development, such as states with high unemployment and low per capita incomes, military procurement spending could be viewed as distributed to affect an important policy problem. If such targeting is related to any of the distributive theories we have discussed, distributive politics could be said to facilitate the effective targeting of military procurement expenditures to places with greater need for economic development.

The above examples make clear that distributive politics and the goal of effective policy making may coincide. In sum, if distributive politics is a way of addressing and solving constituency problems in addition to providing a platform for incumbent advertising and credit claiming, distributive politics may result in local instances of national problems being addressed and conditions improved as well as incumbents getting reelected. Thus we can elaborate on Cain, Ferejohn, and Fiorina's (1987) point that case work and project work are components of the personal vote for a candidate by noting that this may be because real local problems are being addressed and solved. Morever, such activity by reelection-seeking MCs across the country may actually produce effective national targeting and problem solving. Primarily because problem targeting and condition improvement have not been considered aspects of distributive politics, these possibilities have not previously been investigated.

CHAPTER THREE

PREVIOUS STUDIES

Empirical studies of defense policy making in Congress have tended to focus on two kinds of quantitative data: roll call votes from which measures of member ideology can be constructed and census and economic data from which measures of constituency economic interest can be constructed. Roll call data have been used primarily to describe the distribution of hawks and doves in Congress and on defense committees to address the recruitment and outlier or overrepresentation hypotheses. The demographic and economic data have been used primarily to address the benefit hypothesis, an economic interest-based version of the committee outlier hypothesis, and (occasionally) the recruitment hypothesis.

RECRUITMENT HYPOTHESIS

Since the work of Shepsle, Rohde, and others in the 1970s (e.g., Rohde and Shepsle 1973; Shepsle 1978), congressional committee assignments have been understood as investment decisions made on the basis of the benefits these assignments provide to members or legislative groups such as state delegations, legislative parties, and even the whole legislature. Benefits may be characterized in different ways. Individual members, state delegations, or partisan coalitions and their leaders may see benefits as constituency projects or expenditures (Ray 1981). Defense contracts and expenditures, in particular, may bring significant economic benefits to committee members' states in the form of jobs and opportunities for industrial production (Markusen et al. 1991). Consequently, members may seek to protect these economic benefits by maintaining membership on defense committees. This suggests that committee membership is interest driven.

However, Shepsle (1978) found that Armed Services was one of the committees for which it was most difficult to predict freshman committee assignment requests using a measure of constituency interest. For Armed Services, "jurisdiction and constituency interest were most imperfectly matched in the sense that interest variables are less likely to discriminate between applicants and non-applicants" (p. 91). Shepsle (1978: 81) says that "the percent of the district work force in the military or in government employment in the defense area . . . is probably a poor indicator of interest, given the broad and changing nature of Armed Services' jurisdiction." Measurement issues aside, Shepsle concludes that for Armed Services, like all main-line legislative committees, "[t]he matching of assignments to requests, constrained only by scarcity, is both a guiding principle and an accurate description of the committee assignment process" (p. 238). Rohde and Shepsle (1973) report that 30 percent of the Democratic representatives from districts dependent on defense contracting but only 18 percent of other Democrats requested assignment to the House Armed Services Committee. However, Cox and McCubbins (1993: 25) show that this 12 percentage point difference is not statistically significant at the $p < .05$ level. Shepsle (1978) reported that a measure of constituency interest in defense contracting was negatively and significantly related to freshmen's requests for seats on Armed Services. Ray's (1980) analysis of freshman committee assignments in the 1970s found no significant relationship between constituency interest in defense contracting and requests for assignment to the Armed Services Committee.

Arnold (1979) found that during the 1952 to 1976 period, Armed Services attracted a disproportionate number of MCs who had military installations to protect. "Of the ninety-four congressmen who joined between 1953 and 1975, fifty-two (55 percent) represented at least one major Army or Air Force installation, as compared to the 30 to 40 percent of all districts that contained one or more installations" (p. 125). This seems to have resulted in part from additional pressure on MCs to protect local bases during a period of increased base closing activity (p. 126). He concludes that the recruitment effects he identified provide "a good explanation for why Armed Services became unrepresentative of the House in the early 1960s" (p. 127).

Lindsay (1991: 27) contends that representatives seek seats on the House military committees to make good public policy as well as to serve their constituencies. In interviews with new members of these committees in 1971–72 and again in 1981–82, more of those who mentioned a constituency-serving motivation for joining, however, said it had to do with the committees' jurisdiction over installations in their districts than with local military contracting (Lindsay 1991: 27).

What stands out in this brief survey is that substantive interest in defense policy, hawkish ideologies, military bases and employment, and military contracting have all been found in one study or another to be associated with MCs seeking and being granted defense committee membership.

COMMITTEE AS IDEOLOGICAL OUTLIER HYPOTHESIS

Most scholars who have examined the ideological composition of committees conclude that the congressional defense committees in general and the House Armed Services Committee (HASC) in particular are more conservative than their parent chambers (e.g., Goodwin 1970; Hinkley 1975; Krehbiel 1991; but see Goss 1972). Ray (1980b) showed that from 1969 to 1978 House and Senate Armed Service Committee members averaged higher scores on the National Security Index (NSI), a measure of support for the military industrial complex, than did nonmembers. In the House this resulted from the recruitment to the committees of members with higher NSI scores. However, senators recruited to the Armed Services committee had NSI scores that were initially quite similar to those of non-committee Senators. As they served on the Armed Services Committee, however, their scores tended to become more conservative than those of senators not on the Armed Service Committee.

Based on the NSI for the 99th Congress, Krehbiel (1991: 120) shows that, "in the case of Armed Services, . . . [h]igh demanders of defense benefits are more than twice as likely to obtain Armed Services assignments than the average member." This was not true of the Appropriations subcommittees on defense and military construction. He also shows, based on a comparison of Americans for Democratic Action (ADA) scores, that Armed Services is "the most significant conservative outlier, with a median 27.5 points lower (more conservative) than the House's" (p. 128) and that both partisan sides of this committee are more conservative than the average House member (p. 130).

Lindsay reports,

> [From 1969 to 1988] three of the four defense committees averaged significantly higher NSI scores than nonmembers. HASC and SASC [Senate Armed Services Committee] remained much more hawkish than their parent chambers even though several long time critics of DoD—most notably Les Aspin (D-Wis.) and Ron Dellums (D-Calif.)—assumed committee leadership positions in the 1980s. The House Appropriations Defense Subcommittee (HADS) was always more hawkish than the full House[,] . . . even in the 1980s when the dovish Joseph Addabbo (D-N.Y.) chaired the committee.
>
> The average hawkishness of the Senate Appropriations Defense Subcommittee (SADS) differs from the other three committees. . . . [From 1975 to 1984] SADS registered mean NSI ratings fairly close to those of nonmembers. The Legislative Reorganization Act of 1970 accounts for the difference. . . . The

law limited future senators to only one seat on the Senate's top four committees—Appropriations, Armed Services, Finance, and Foreign Relations. . . . [This] broke the grip that a small group of conservative (and Hawkish) senators held on major committee assignments. (1991: 24)

Cox and McCubbins (1993) show that the Democratic contingent on Armed Services has tended to be ideologically unrepresentative of House Democrats for most of the post–World War II period. They also say, "Although these results are broadly consistent with the predictions of the partisan selection model, they are also consistent with self-selection, so they can hardly be taken as definitive" (p. 229). Moreover, "Armed Services was atypical of most committees in receiving more support from Republicans than from Democrats in six of nine Congresses (p. 266) and has been "out of control from the [Democratic] majority party's viewpoint" (p. 268).

In sum, there is evidence that the House Armed Services Committee is usually an ideological outlier. Although other defense committees have been studied less often, they too appear to be ideological outliers at least in some congresses.

COMMITTEE AS INTEREST OUTLIER HYPOTHESIS

Goss (1972) reports that in 1968 districts represented on the HASC averaged 14,030 military employees as compared with the House average of 6,041. She concludes that membership on this committee was associated with high levels of base employment but that it was not linked to employment at private defense plants (p. 224).

However, Arnold (1979: 105) points out that although Armed Services Committee members' districts always averaged more army and air force personnel than did nonmembers' districts from 1952 to 1974, the 1968 figure reported by Goss (1972) represented the largest difference in that period. Arnold (1979: 105) also shows that the defense and military construction subcommittees of Appropriations were fairly representative of the whole House in terms of the number of military employees in members' districts.

Adler and Lapinski (1997: 910) contend that "[t]he Armed Services Committee . . . attracts members who have large or important military installations with sizeable numbers of personnel in their districts." In their study, Armed Services Committee members' constituency need scores tended to be statistically different from the floor. However, Cox and McCubbins (1993) make a good case that overrecruitment and overrepresentation of defense committee members from defense contracting areas was nonexistent, even during the Rayburn-era congresses that Sheple studied.

Thus, like the research on recruitment to defense committees, there is mixed evidence that defense committees overrepresent districts with a measurable interest in defense spending beyond the presence of military installations.

BENEFIT HYPOTHESIS

The hypothesis that committee members are able to influence military decisions so that their constituencies benefit has been explored in a number of previous studies (e.g., Rundquist and Ferejohn 1975). MCs, operating from such a parochial perspective, "review a weapons system in terms of how it affects the job prospects of constituents. . . . What matters is where a weapon will be built and where it will be based" (Lindsay 1991: 12–13)

Arnold (1979) investigated whether constituencies represented on the HASC benefited by being less likely to suffer a base closure. His multivariate probit analysis of army and air force base closures showed that installations without representation on the military committees were more than twice as likely to be closed as those with committee representation (p. 113). He found a similar effect of committee representation on the likelihood that new installations would be built in a district (p. 118). However, he uncovered no support for the hypothesis that committee members were able to increase employment at local installations (p. 120). Arnold's military employment model included six variables for each installation: committee representation, current employment level, change in national military employment, change in national employment for particular military functions, change in the number of installations in existence, and the installation's age. He also conducted a district-level rather than installation-level analysis that showed no committee effects on local employment levels.

Regarding the hypothesis that committee representation helps districts to retain or increase their benefit level from year to year, Ray (1980a) reported that between 1969 and 1976, a period that includes the end of the Vietnam war, congressional districts represented on defense committees were no less likely to suffer decreases in total defense department expenditures than districts not represented on these committees. The expenditure variable in this study was the year-to-year change in DOD spending (in constant dollars) by district, using Office of Economic Opportunity compilations from 1968 to 1977.

Arnold's (1979) evidence on the same issue is mixed. Committee member's districts suffered fewer air force base closures but about the same number of army base closures during the period 1952–74. He also reported a negative bivariate correlation between committee representation and changes in employment at military installations, suggesting that committee representation resulted in greater than average losses in employment (p. 32), perhaps because committee members' districts had more military employment to lose.

Finally, Dering (1998) suggests that committee representation alone is not enough to cause constituencies to benefit. In the 1980s and 1990s, it appears that the Defense Department used base closings as an opportunity to punish liberal defense committee members by targeting bases in their districts for closure.

PARTY HYPOTHESIS

Studies of partisan effects on the distribution of federal benefits are fairly recent, perhaps because political scientists have heeded Lowi's (1964) argument that political parties were more active in regulatory and redistributive policy making than in distributive policy making. Studies of committee effects often distinguish between Democrats and Republicans or note that Democrats have generally been the majority party during the period under study, but the possibility that Democrats might benefit more than Republicans because of their majority status has seldom been examined. Levitt and Snyder's (1995) study of domestic program outlays is an exception. They tested several party hypotheses, finding that federal domestic expenditures tend to be distributed disproportionately to districts with large numbers of Democratic voters. This effect also applies to formula-based programs and is stronger for programs with smaller, more geographically concentrated benefits. They also find that programs initiated under Democratic control in the mid- to late 1970s evidence this pro-Democratic bias most strongly, while programs initiated under Ronald Reagan show little pro-Democratic bias. Bickers, Sellers, and Stein (1996) also report a partisan effect on domestic policy making, finding that Democrats and Republicans tend to seek and obtain different sorts of benefits. Democratic districts tend to benefit more from grant programs, whereas Republican districts benefit more from loan programs.

Looking specifically at the role of partisanship in defense spending, Ray showed that there is a tendency for Republicans on the Armed Services Committees to have higher NSI scores than committee Democrats:

> [T]he Armed Service Committees are not much more bipartisan than Congress as a whole. . . . Armed Services Democrats are considerably more "dovish" than are Committee Republicans, and on both panels this disparity has been growing, although much faster in the Senate. Moreover, as in the parent institutions, the standard deviations reveal that Democrats are much less homogenous in their support for national security issues than are members of the GOP. In both parties, however, Committee members, on average, are more supportive of the military industrial complex than are Committee non-members. (1980c: 513)

Cox and McCubbins (1993: 182) show that among Democrats, party loyalty (voting with the majority leader on roll call votes) affects whether members' requests for committee transfers are honored. "This of course makes committees and their members more responsive to both the party's leadership and goals" (p. 182). Party loyalty in their first term also plays a role in the committee assignments given to newly elected representatives (p. 186), although a significant exception to this tendency is the appointees to Armed Services (p. 185).

We noted in chapter 2 that the various distributive theories may work in combination with each other rather than separately. Shepsle and Weingast (1995: 30) and Cox and McCubbins (1993) suggest that party effects may combine with committee effects to influence the distribution of benefits. Goss (1972: 224) observes that in defense policy, "[a]pparently it is not simply committee membership that is linked to high levels of base employment, but *Democratic* committee membership" (original emphasis).

> The conclusion is inescapable that high average employment at military bases is associated with committee membership and Democratic affiliation. Since the Democrats have controlled Congress during most of the cold war era of heavy defense spending, one inference that could be drawn is that committee Democrats exercised influence in bringing bases to their districts and keeping them there. (Goss 1972: 225)

Thus, for some types of defense spending, party loyalty and partisanship have been shown to be important causal variables. There is also evidence that they do not operate independently of committee and ideology. However, how they affect military procurement spending is unclear.

IDEOLOGY HYPOTHESIS

Several scholars have argued that ideology structures congressional policy making in general (e.g., Poole and Rosenthal 1997) and defense policy making in particular (e.g., Moyer 1973; Bernstein and Anthony 1974; Fleisher 1985; Lindsay 1991). Most of these studies find that MC ideology correlates more strongly with MC voting on defense policy than do constituency factors. In other words, MCs vote hawkishly or dovishly on defense spending independent of the interest their constituencies may have in receiving defense expenditures. Kau and Rubin (1982) describe this as MCs shirking their constituencies' economic interests in favor of following their individual ideological predispositions. Lindsay states,

> The first and foremost reason why Congress does not lead on nuclear issues has to do with the strength of hawks in both the House and Senate. . . . [H]awks constituted a near majority in both the House and Senate during the Ninety-first through Hundreth Congresses. Many fewer doves . . . sit in Congress, although their number grew in the House during the 1980s. (1991: 116)

More generally, Jackson and Kingdon state,

> We do not disagree with the notion that legislators' votes reflect, at least in part, their own world view about what is good policy. Indeed, we are convinced that ideology is an important influence on governmental decisions. (1992: 806)

However, Jackson and Kingdon go on to argue that research on the role of ideology in Congress has been seriously flawed, primarily because both the independent variable, in this case hawkish or dovish ideology, and the dependent variables, support for or opposition to aggressive defense policies and spending on weapons systems, have been measured with roll call votes or vote indexes that tend to be highly correlated. They argue that this misuse of roll call votes tends to undermine the conclusions of most scholars regarding the role of personal ideology.

Lindsay points to a similar problem:

The considerable statistical evidence that members' general defense views or ideology best predict how they vote may simply reflect the fact that legislators vote on the basis of constituency opinion. (1991: 116)

However, he notes that most of the votes used to construct the National Security Index on which this conclusion is based did not concern issues in which constituency benefits were at stake and therefore were likely to reflect "ideology" rather than "constituency interests." But to the extent that roll call votes tend to load on a single ideological dimension (Poole and Rosenthal 1997), Jackson and Kingdon's argument would still apply.

The issue of what constitutes MC ideology and its separation from constituency characteristics forces us to deal with our findings regarding MC ideology with caution. However, our analysis does not suffer from Jackson and Kingdon's criticism that MC ideology and the dependent variable(s) it is assumed to predict are both measured using MC roll call votes. As we describe more fully in chapter 4, our measure of ideology is based on roll call votes, but our dependent variable is the distribution of military procurement expenditures and not congressional support for specific defense programs.

UNIVERSALISM HYPOTHESES

Most evidence of universalism in defense policy comes from roll call voting on omnibus military procurement bills. Studies find that most military procurement bills pass with super- majority support (Collie 1988; Lindsay 1991). The evidence for universalism, either intra- or interpolicy universalism, in military contracting data is fairly thin. Several studies conclude that universalism exists when tests of the committee- centered hypothesis are not supported (e.g., Arnold 1979). In this view, evidence that committee, party, or ideology does not influence the geographic distribution of policy benefits is seen as evidence of universalism. In a study of subcontracting for nine major prime military contracts, Mayer (1991: chap.

6) finds little evidence of subcontracting benefits being targeted to committee members' districts and states. Instead, he concludes that there is considerable evidence of universalism in the wide spread of subcontracts among the states. He interprets this as evidence that the Pentagon builds congressional support for its weapons systems by making sure that many MCs receive something. But he argues that a full test of this conjecture is impossible because too little subcontracting data are available.

Crump and Archer (1993) present an analysis that may be read as suggesting that defense expenditures are distributed consistent with inter- rather than intrapolicy universalism. They report:

> [I]t has been found that while defense outlays do tend to favor counties in coastal defense perimeter states, the opposite is true of non-defense outlays, which tend to favor counties in interior non-perimeter states. Moreover, when defense and non-defense outlays are summed to obtain total outlays per capita at county level in 1989, the diminutive average difference is found to be too small to be statistically significant. (P. 60)

In other words, Crump and Archer suggest that places that receive disproportionately more defense spending are those that receive disproportionately less nondefense spending. This supports the idea that cross-policy logrolling may be taking place. However, they also say,

> [T]he county-level geographical distributions of defense and non-defense outlays are very unlike one another for the nation as a whole. Indeed, total defense and total non-defense expenditures exhibit locational patterns which are essentially statistically independent, as shown by a correlation coefficient of just 0.054 between the county-level distributions of per capita defense and non-defense outlays during FY-1989. (P. 60).

This contradicts the idea that logrolling occurs between defense and nondefense expenditures, for if that were the case, the correlation they are describing should be *negative* and significant. This is supported by others who conclude that the committee-centered logrolling version of the distributive theory cannot account for military construction spending. According to Soherr-Hadwiger,

> [c]ongressional voting on seven milcon bills does not support the economic model of voting advanced by universalism theorists. Distributive benefits clearly influence legislators' voting on omnibus bills, but this is not the only factor influencing these votes, and it may not be the most important. (1998: 75)

CRITIQUE

The studies of particular distributive politics hypotheses regarding military procurement and other types of defense spending have covered different time periods, used a variety of research designs and statistical methods, examined specific hypotheses in isolation from other possibly related hypotheses, and focused on different dependent variables or different measures of the same dependent variable. Therefore, it is not surprising that these studies have reached several, sometimes conflicting conclusions. While some distributive politics research has examined the correlates of targeting defense contracts and some researchers have controlled for economic capacity in their targeting studies, none have examined the effectiveness and economic impact of defense spending and the distributive politics thereof. Although the previous research is suggestive of the form that a more comprehensive quantitative study of the distributive politics of military procurement spending might take, our review of this literature indicates two primary reasons why there has been little consensus regarding distributive politics.

First, there has been inadequate theoretical development of alternative distributive theories. The problem of how a distributive politics of military procurement spending might work under different political, economic, and strategic conditions has not been stated in a comprehensive way. Therefore, researchers have examined only isolated hypotheses rather than more complete analytic models of distributive politics that allow for multiple, possibly interrelated hypotheses to be tested.

The second reason relates to the first but is primarily methodological rather than theoretical. Most research designs employed in the literature are not capable of testing a more comprehensive statistical model of distributive politics. Obviously, studies that include a limited set of potentially relevant variables cannot adequately test the various competing theories of distributive politics outlined in chapter 2. Furthermore, because we contend that a number of conditional, or interactive, effects may exist and that the factors we have discussed may be linked in reciprocal relationships, a research design that allows for their examination is required. Finally, to the extent that distributive politics unfolds dynamically over time, cross-sectional designs are inappropriate. We close this chapter by paying more specific attention to research design issues.

RESEARCH DESIGN ISSUES

1) Change in policy benefits. Almost all defense spending studies have been of the level of programmatic activity (usually expenditures) in constituencies, not of the change in the level that could be produced by distributive politics in any particular Congress. Cross-sectional research designs prevent modeling the dynamic nature of distributive politics, yet it is change in the existing distribution of benefits that distributive theories predict. We address programmatic change by using a pooled time-series analysis. This allows us to specify a statistical model that isolates the influence of each independent variable on changes in levels of military procurement expenditures going to localities, changes in defense committee representation, and changes in state economic conditions.

2) Cumulative effects. That most empirical studies have employed cross-sectional designs also prevents consideration of how the effects of distributive politics might accumulate over time.[1] It is consistent with theories of distributive politics that this cumulative effect may be in part what MCs are trying to create, either for

the good of the constituency or to insulate themselves from electoral challenge. The pooled time-series analysis and our focus on modeling change over time allow us to examine the accumulation of military procurement awards.

3) Reciprocal relationships. Most distributive politics studies have failed to unravel the reciprocal relationship between the geographic distribution of policy benefits among places and whether a place is represented on relevant congressional committees. Do areas that benefit from defense contracting subsequently obtain defense committee representation (recruitment hypothesis), or do areas represented on defense committees subsequently obtain additional defense expenditures (benefit hypothesis)? Shepsle (1978: 82) notes an important aspect of an MC's "interest" in getting on the Armed Services Committee that is ignored in most studies of committee recruitment: "Requests need not be conditioned by *prior* interest—members, that is, may to some extent convert committee membership into *future* pork benefits for their districts" (original emphasis). Similarly, most studies of the committee-induced benefit hypothesis combine the level of contracts or bases that were already in the constituency and that may have led the member to have joined a defense committee in the first place with the level of procurement contracts that committee membership may have independently stimulated.

Almost all empirical studies have used single equation models to examine the relationship between committee representation and the allocation of benefits. However, depending on the specification of the model (i.e., which variable is modeled as the dependent variable and which as the independent variable[s]), evidence of a positive relationship between benefit distribution and committee representation has been interpreted either as committee members reacting to constituency demand or as committee members proactively directing benefits (pork) back home regardless of demand. We propose a multiequation model to sort out this "chicken-and-egg" problem.

4) Direct and indirect effects of distributive politics. Failure to model the reciprocal relationship between the geographic distri-

bution of military benefits and whether a state is represented on a defense committee also prevents scholars from considering both direct and indirect effects. Consider the following hypothetical situation. Suppose analysis reveals that states represented by defense committee members receive disproportionately larger increases in military procurement spending but that states represented by relatively more conservative MCs do not. One might conclude from this that committee, not ideology, structures the distributive politics of military procurement spending. However, suppose that further research reveals that states represented by more conservative MCs have a greater probability of being represented on a defense committee. We could then conclude that ideology does influence the distribution of military procurement benefits but *indirectly* by working through defense committee representation. The distinction between direct and indirect effects has not been made in previous studies. The multiequation approach to modeling potential reciprocal relationships facilitates the examination of direct and indirect effects of distributive politics.

5) Effectiveness and impact. We have already noted that most studies of distributive politics make assumptions about its effectiveness but rarely test those assumptions. Similarly, scholars have considered the economic impact of defense spending at the national (Russett 1970; Sandler and Hartley 1995) and state (Brace 1993) levels. However, such studies have not examined systematically the contribution distributive politics makes to creating these impacts. Correcting this problem first requires including measures of a state's capacity to convert military procurement benefits into the goods needed for the national defense and measures of a state's economic condition. Of course, it also requires addressing policy change, cumulative benefits, reciprocal relationships, and indirect effects as they relate to the targeting of military procurement expenditures.

CHAPTER FOUR

A MODEL OF
DISTRIBUTIVE POLITICS

In this chapter, we present a series of three figures designed to highlight the central features of distributive politics suggested by the competing theories outlined in chapter 2. The figures illustrate the analytic model of distributive politics that we examine in subsequent chapters, but as will be seen, they represent an oversimplification. In particular, they fail to show a number of possible conditional or interactive relationships that previous theoretical and empirical work suggest are important to be considered.

We begin with a simple committee-based model, shown in figure 4.1. We have argued previously that there is a reciprocal relationship between the geographic distribution of military spending across states and whether a state is represented on a defense committee (Carsey and Rundquist 1999b). By "reciprocal" we mean that MCs on defense committees are hypothesized to proactively direct military spending back to their home states at a disproportionately higher rate than do noncommittee MCs (the committee benefit hypothesis), while at the same time states that receive relatively higher levels of defense spending are more likely to acquire subsequent representation on a defense committee (the committee recruitment hypothesis).

Although defense committee representation and the distribution of military spending are interrelated, these causal effects should not

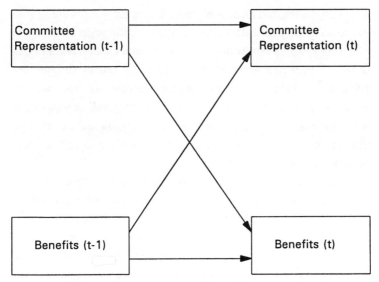

Fig. 4.1. Basic model of distributive politics.

be expected to occur simultaneously. Rather the reciprocal process unfolds over time. Representation on a defense committee in one year is not expected to affect benefit levels for those states until the following year. Similarly, relatively high levels of benefits in one year cannot push MCs to seek membership on a defense committee until the following year at the earliest.

Another central component of the model is the incremental nature by which change takes place. Current levels of procurement spending in a state depend in part on the previous year's level of spending. Similarly, the likelihood that a state is represented on a defense committee in a given year depends on whether that state was represented on a defense committee in the previous year. Focusing first on military procurement awards, the allocation of defense contract dollars never changes completely from one year to the next. Instead each year's allocation of defense contract dollars is based in part on the previous year's allocation. Change from one year to the next is incremental. In more technical terms, what we are saying is that the distribution of per capita military procurement expenditures follows an autoregressive process: what states got in one year carries over into influencing which states get what in the following year. By controlling for the previous year's level of per capita military procurement expenditures in our model, we are able to focus our attention on whether other factors are related to *changes* in per capita military procurement spending that occur from one year to the next. Also, by modeling the autoregressive process, our model allows us to generate estimates of the accumulation of benefits over time.

Committee representation is also characterized by an autoregressive process. Once MCs are appointed to a defense committee, they have a tendency to remain on the committee from one year to the next. This results in part from the advantage incumbents have in obtaining reelection and the subsequent use of seniority as a major criterion for selecting committee leaders. The seniority system gives members an incentive to stay on the committees to which they were previously appointed. Thus an important determinant of whether a state is represented on a defense committee in either chamber of Congress is whether that state was so represented in the previous year. Our model is structured to uncover the effect of factors that might be related to *changes* in defense committee representation.

Figure 4.1 illustrates the basic process we have described so far. To simplify the presentation, we assume that the same basic structure of distributive politics applies to both chambers of Congress. This does not necessarily mean that the fit of the model will be identical in both chambers. When we test the model statistically, we will evaluate its empirical fit for the House and the Senate separately.[1]

To summarize, figure 4.1 shows how the distribution of military benefits and representation on a defense committee may be reciprocally related. Prior representation on a defense committee is expected to cause changes in the level of benefits allocated to a state, and previous levels of military spending in a state influence the chances of the state being represented on a defense committee.

The time subscripts "t-1" and "t" make it clear that these relationships unfold over time. Figure 4.1 also shows that both committee representation and the distribution of benefits are hypothesized to change incrementally (they each depend on their own previous values). The figure illustrates the prediction that deviations from the trend in committee representation are expected to respond to the prior distribution of benefits. At the same time, changes in the pattern of benefit allocation are expected to respond to whether a state was represented on a defense committee in the previous year.

The next step is to add competing explanations for the distribution of policy benefits and who is represented on the defense committees. Figure 4.2 does this by including partisanship and ideology. "Ideology" refers to the average ideological orientation of a state's delegation to Congress. The figure suggests that if MC ideology drives the distributive politics of defense spending, states with relatively more conservative delegations should be more likely to gain representation on defense committees, and those same states should be more likely to receive increases in their level of defense spending. Figure 4.2 shows that this effect would appear after controlling for prior committee representation and benefit levels.

"Partisanship" represents the partisan makeup of a state's delegation, or the proportion of a state's delegation that consists of MCs from the majority party. The figure suggests that partisanship might have a direct influence on the likelihood that a state will subsequently be represented on a defense committee as well as on the level of defense benefits a state receives. This direct, or pure, party effect would be expected to appear if the distributive politics of defense spending is dominated by the majority party in Congress with the goal of serving the interests of all majority party MCs.

Thus figure 4.2 presents a fairly complete, if somewhat simplified, illustration of distributive politics that allows for committee representation, partisanship, and ideology to compete with each other to influence both defense committee representation and the distribution of military procurement benefits. As presented, analysis of a model based on figure 4.2 would not be predisposed to

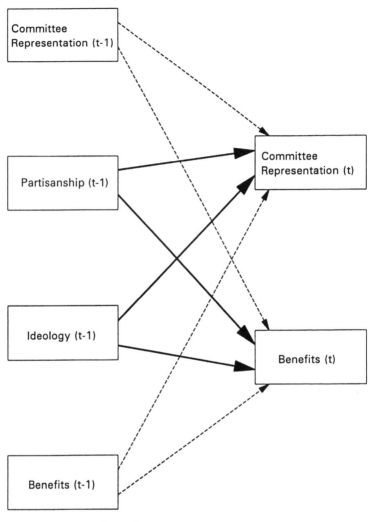

----- = basic model from figure 4.1.
——— = additions to figure 4.1.

Fig. 4.2. Adding party and ideology to the model.

uncover evidence supporting any one of the leading interpretations of distributive politics over the others. Rather it provides for a fair assessment of the importance of each potentially influential factor in predicting the distribution of benefits and defense committee representation. When we test a statistical model based on this figure using data from 1963 to 1995, we will be able to evaluate the influence of each factor during this time period, examine whether the relative influence of these factors changes over time, and examine whether an increase in the importance of one factor in predicting defense committee representation and/or the distribution of military procurement expenditures is associated with an increase or decrease in the importance of one or more of the other factors.

Not shown in figure 4.2, but considered in our subsequent analysis, is whether the effects of committee representation, partisanship, and ideology interact with each other to influence changes in the distribution of benefits or representation on a defense committee. Our previous work (Carsey and Rundquist 1999a) uncovered evidence that partisanship interacts with prior committee representation to influence subsequent committee representation and the targeting of defense benefits. In other words, it may be that the combination of majority party representation *and* having that majority party representation on a defense committee results in subsequent or continued representation on defense committees and/or additional benefits being distributed to a state. In the analysis presented in this book, we test a complete set of interactions between committee, party, and ideology. We do not illustrate these potential interactive effects in figure 4.2 because doing so would obscure the basic structure of the distributive theories we are describing here.

Figure 4.2 lacks a concern for the effectiveness and economic impact of the distributive politics of military procurement. In figure 4.3, we correct this omission by adding measures of relative economic conditions and industrial capacity at time t-1 as predictors of committee representation and benefits at time t, and also by adding a measure of subsequent economic conditions at Time t+1 to assess whether receiving benefits in the previous year had a measurable impact on economic growth in a state.

As we have argued previously, the distribution of policy benefits can be said to be effective from a national defense perspective if it successfully directs funds to places where the capacity for doing defense work is higher. As a secondary issue, defense procurement awards targeted to places in greater relative need of economic stimulation could indicate effectiveness in meeting the need for economic development. We can assess the economic impact of defense procurement first by measuring the direct effect of military procurement contracts on subsequent economic conditions. If there is economic growth associated with higher levels of defense procurement expenditures, we can determine whether this results in rich states getting richer by looking back at whether relatively wealthy states receive a disproportionate share of procurement expenditures. One might also examine whether the distribution of defense procurement expenditures has any impact on a state's industrial capacity, although using a general measure of capacity such as gross state product (GSP) due to manufacturing reduces the likelihood of uncovering an effect.[2] Figure 4.3 shows the direct relationships between economic conditions and capacity measured at time t-1 and the distribution of benefits that results at time t. Should these direct effects be evident, they could be interpreted as resulting from a process in which policy benefits are directed to places on the basis of economic need and/or capacity. This would constitute evidence that the distribution of miliary procurement funds is effective. Furthermore, figure 4.3 shows how a direct effect of procurement benefits distributed at time t may influence economic conditions in the following year, t+1.

It is also possible that both the direct effects of distributive politics and effective targeting are at work but that they may constitute competing pressures on the distribution of military procurement awards. In this case, we might also see significant over-time variation in the effects of the two types of variables. For example,

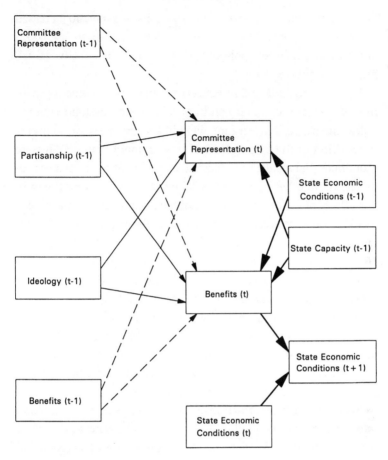

----- = base model from figure 4.1.
——— = additions to figure 4.2.

Fig. 4.3. Adding effectiveness to the model.

one might suspect that in times of military conflict, more procurement benefits might be targeted to higher-capacity states regardless of defense committee representation, partisanship, or ideology. In contrast, peacetime defense procurement may be more subject to committee, party, or ideological pressures.

Another scenario is that previous levels of economic need or capacity influence the probability of a state obtaining representation on a defense committee, which may in turn translate into increased military procurement benefits. If this is the case, then one could argue that distributive politics itself facilitates the effective distribution of policy benefits.

Figure 4.3 includes a direct effect of military procurement expenditures on state economic conditions. However, by following the paths illustrated in the figure, we will also be able to account for the portion of the direct effect of procurement benefits on state economies that results from the distributive politics of defense procurement. In other words, we will be able to account for the indirect effects of factors such as committee representation, party, and ideology on state economic conditions as they influence (or do not influence) the distribution of military procurement expenditures. For example, suppose we find that representation on a House defense committee leads to relatively larger changes in military procurement expenditures being distributed to a state. Suppose further that military procurement expenditures lead to increases in state per capita incomes. If so, we will be able to describe the indirect effect of House defense committee representation on growth in state per capita incomes as it works through the geographic distribution of military procurement benefits.

Recalling the basic structure of distributive politics presented in figure 4.1, also embedded in figure 4.3, a more general statement regarding distributive politics can be made. Figure 4.1 suggests that committee representation and the distribution of benefits are reciprocally related and that both change incrementally. If this proves to be the case, then any factor that has a direct influence on *either* committee representation or the distribution of policy benefits will subsequently have an indirect effect on *both* committee representation and the distribution of benefits. Furthermore, any onetime effect of a factor on defense committee representation or on the distribution of defense procurement benefits will continue to influence committee representation and the distribution of benefits over time due to the autoregressive nature of these processes. For example, if ideology directly influences committee representation and committee representation directly influences benefits, then over time ideology indirectly influences the distribution of benefits. Furthermore, that indirect effect will continue to affect the distribution of defense benefits in subsequent years because change in the distribution of benefits happens incrementally.

Figure 4.3 presents a simplified but comprehensive illustration of distributive politics that allows for a number of factors to influence committee representation and the distribution of benefits. It remains to be seen which, if any, of the hypothesized relationships shown receive empirical support in the area of military procurement spending. The next step is to translate the relationships illustrated in figure 4.3 into a set of equations that permit empirical evaluation. Table 4.1 presents a set of such equations. Note that in table 4.1 i refers to individual places (states) and t refers to a particular point in time (year). When actually estimated, we divide equation (2) into separate equations for the House and Senate, but note here that we already take into account the two separate chambers of Congress on the right-hand side of each equation.[3] Equation (3) is also separated into two equations to measure the impact of defense procurement expenditures on state per capita incomes and state levels of unemployment. When the analysis is performed, the equations are estimated simultaneously and the error terms for all of the equations are allowed to be contemporaneously correlated.

Each equation includes a lagged value of the dependent variable as a predictor of that variable. When an equation includes a lagged value of the dependent variable as a regressor, it is proper to think of the remaining independent variables as having (or not having) an effect on *change* in the dependent variable from one time period to the next (Finkel 1995). The coefficients operating on the lagged values of the dependent variables in each equation capture the autoregressive nature of the distributive process and are expected to be positive and significant. Anything that affects one of the dependent variables at some point in time will be felt for a number of time periods that follow because of the autoregressive nature of each time series. This allows us to capture the dynamics

TABLE 4.1.

Statistical Model of the Distributive Process

(1) $\text{Benefits}_{it} = \alpha_1 + \beta_1(\text{Benefits}_{it-1}) + \beta_2(\text{Democratic House Committee Rep}_{it-1}) + \beta_3(\text{Republican House Committee Rep}_{it-1}) + \beta_4(\text{Democratic Senate Committee Rep}_{it-1}) + \beta_5(\text{Republican Senate Committee Rep}_{it-1}) + \beta_6(\text{House Partisanship}_{it-1}) + \beta_7(\text{Senate Partisanship}_{it-1}) + \beta_8(\text{House Delegation Ideology}_{it-1}) + \beta_9(\text{Senate Delegation Ideology}_{it-1}) + \beta_{10}(\text{Capacity}_{it-1}) + \beta_{11}(\text{Economic Conditions}_{it-1}) + e1_{it}$

(2) $\text{Committee Representation}_{it} = \alpha_2 + \beta_{12}(\text{Benefits}_{it-1}) + \beta_{13}(\text{Democratic House Committee Rep}_{it-1}) + \beta_{14}(\text{Republican House Committee Rep}_{it-1}) + \beta_{15}(\text{Democratic Senate Committee Rep}_{it-1}) + \beta_{16}(\text{Republican Senate Committee Rep}_{it-1}) + \beta_{17}(\text{House Partisanship}_{it-1}) + \beta_{18}(\text{Senate Partisanship}_{it-1}) + \beta_{19}(\text{House Delegation Ideology}_{it-1}) + \beta_{20}(\text{Senate Delegation Ideology}_{it-1}) + \beta_{21}(\text{Capacity}_{it-1}) + \beta_{22}(\text{Economic Conditions}_{it-1}) + e2_{it}$

(3) $\text{Economic Conditions}_{it} = \alpha_3 + \beta_{23}(\text{Benefits}_{it-1}) + \beta_{24}(\text{Economic Conditions}_{it-1}) + e3_{it}$

NOTE: The subscript *it* refers to individual states at particular points in time. Because of the pooled nature of the data, equations (1) and (3) include a set of region and year dummy variables. Equation (2) includes only the region dummies. Further information on the estimation of models based on the one presented in this table can be found in Appendix A.

of the distributive process and to consider how effects in the model accumulate over time.

Finally, when we actually evaluate the model against data, we consider a number of potential interactive effects among the independent variables in the various equations. By "interactive effects," we mean, for example, the potential that party, committee, or ideology work in combination to influence the distribution of military procurement awards. We explore these possibilities using a variety of multiplicative interaction terms.[4] We considered a number of such possibilities, although in the following chapters we present only those findings for which we uncovered some evidence.

To summarize, the basic structure of the statistical model meets several important criteria. It allows us to estimate the dynamic nature of distributive politics. It captures the influence of independent variables on *change* in committee representation and the distribution of defense procurement awards. It allows us to consider how effects might accumulate over time. Finally, it allows us to test simultaneously the potential direct and interactive effects of competing versions of the distributive theory along with the effectiveness of the process.

HYPOTHESES

Having constructed a statistical model of the distributive process that incorporates central variables from a number of distributive theories of politics, we can now present the hypotheses that are tested in subsequent chapters.

- If Congress allocates benefits to places with the greatest economic need, we should find a direct positive effect of need on benefits in equation (1).
- If Congress allocates benefits to places with the highest defense production capacity, we should see a direct positive effect of capacity on benefits in equation (1).
- If committee representation facilitates either of these processes, we should find a positive effect of need and/or

capacity on committee representation in equation (2) as well as a positive effect of committee representation on benefits in equation (1).

- If the allocation of benefits alleviates economic need, we should see a negative relationship between benefits and need in equation (3).

- If MCs are able to direct benefits to their constituents via the committee structure, then committee representation should have a positive effect on benefits after controlling for economic need in equation (1).

- Further, if economic need does not influence committee representation in equation (2), then the resulting benefits directed back to constituents by committee members represents ineffective targeting, or pork barrel politics.

- If distributive politics is purely party centered rather than committee centered, places represented by majority party members should receive greater benefits in equation (1) regardless of committee representation.

- If the distributive process is committee based but structured by the majority party, the effects of committee representation on benefits in equation (1) should be stronger for majority party MCs.

- If committee representation provides majority party MCs with more power to direct benefits back to their constituents and if the majority party has greater control over the structure of the committee system, we should see areas represented by majority party MCs on defense committees better able to retain that representation than areas represented by minority party members.

- If MCs protect benefits once they have been allocated, representation on defense committees should respond positively to past values of benefits in equation (2).

- If intrapolicy universalism holds, then we would expect a roughly equal distribution of military procurement benefits across states and that committee, party, and ideology would not be related to changes in that distribution.

- If interpolicy universalism holds, we would expect to see within this one policy area effects that mirror the pure committee-centered distributive theory.
- If the distribution of military procurement expenditures is structured by MCs' ideology, we should see a significant relationship between ideology and benefits in equation (1). Ideology would also be expected to predict committee representation in equation (2).

RESEARCH DESIGN

The comprehensive statistical model of the distributive process presented above allows for party, committee, and ideological effects and also assesses the effectiveness of distributive politics. Here we describe the data we use to test this model, along with a number of methodological issues raised by our approach.

Unit of Analysis

We carry out our study at the state level. Typically, studies that test distributive hypotheses have analyzed data at the state or district level, although neither has been determined to be more appropriate (Rundquist and Ferejohn 1975; Rundquist, Lee, and Rhee, 1996). The utility of county-level analysis has also been demonstrated (Anton, Hawley, and Kramer 1980; Heitshusen 1991; Rundquist et al. 1997). At the county level, "[f]ederal program outlays are closely associated with 'need' in programs designed to address those needs" (Anton, Hawley, and Kramer 1980: 78). We chose the state level for several reasons.

First, more data are available for the variables that make up our statistical model of distributive politics at the state level than at any other. In particular, measuring the geographic location of federal military expenditures before the 1980s is possible only at the state level. By looking at states, we are able to span more than thirty years and include the significant buildups of the late 1960s and early 1980s as well as the build-downs that followed. As our findings show, the distributive politics of military procurement is dynamic, changing over time in response to changing environmental circumstances. Illustrating this aspect of distributive politics requires data over a longer period.

Second, state boundaries do not change every ten years as do congressional district boundaries. Studies at the congressional-district level have been severely limited in scope because of their inability to transcend each decennial census and the redistricting that results. Conducting the analysis at the state level avoids this problem.

Third, states constitute meaningful political subdivisions in the United States. Representation in the Senate is defined by state borders. Presidential elections are determined by state electoral votes. States have been shown to have unique political cultures (Elazar 1984), political ideologies (Erickson, Wright, and McIver 1993), and party systems (Brown 1995). Obviously, the outcome of presidential contests varies across states, but the factors that influence voter preferences in presidential elections and party identification also vary across states (Jackson and Carsey 1999a, 1999b). More specifically, state delegations in Congress often work and vote together on matters of common interest in their state (Deckard 1972; Levitt and Snyder 1995; Van der Slik 1995; Bickers and Stein 1996, 1999).

Fourth, states have been used as units of analysis in previous studies of defense politics and policy. Besides our own work (Carsey and Rundquist 1999a, 1999b), Markusen, and colleagues (1991) compare the distribution of military contracts among states during the twentieth century. Trubowitz's (1998) study of the regional coalitions that produced American defense policy in the 1890s, 1930s, and 1980s focuses on the percentage of each state delegation that supports military expansion proposals in each period. In addition, scholars of state economic development often control for federal defense expenditures knowing that such factors may have an important influence on states (e.g., Brace 1993). In short, there are a number of both substantive and methodological reasons to support conducting this analysis at the state level.

There are, of course, limitations to using states as the unit of analysis. Representation in the House is organized by congressional districts, not states. This would lead some to argue that given distributive theory's focus on the incentives of MCs, distributive politics would be better modeled for House members at the district level (but see Levitt and Snyder 1995). This is reasonable but also places major limitations on any study of distributive politics. As mentioned, redistricting greatly limits the ability of scholars to study more than a ten-year period. Also, measures of military procurement spending do not exist at the district level. They must be created using existing county-level data. This involves making a series of assumptions about how to treat the numerous districts that make up large urban counties and how do deal with counties that are divided into more than one district. The first problem results in such urban districts being measured as receiving the same amount of expenditures when we know that cannot be true. The second problem can be resolved by dividing expenditures received in a county among the various districts of which it is a part in proportion to the distribution of the county's population among this districts, but again we know that cannot be true. Both problems introduce measurement error, with the first clearly reducing variance in the expenditure variable relative to other variables that can be measured at the district level. Thus it is not clear that a district-level analysis would produce more accurate estimates of distributive politics in the House. Predictions from distributive theories to characteristics of states such as committee representation and benefit levels can be made and have been made in the literature. If anything, aggregation to the state level should dampen any effects that might exist in the House. This represents a bias against finding significant distributive effects in our analysis as it relates to the House. Yet, as we show in the following chapters, we still do.

One might be able to make a better case for county-level analysis than analysis of congressional districts. Redistricting does not pose problems here, but data availability does. County-level measures of military procurement spending exist only back to 1983. Furthermore, it is not clear that using counties as the unit of analysis is appropriate for questions related to Senate representation and, in some cases, representation in the House. Neither chamber's representation is based on counties, and the size and composition of counties varies tremendously both within states and across them. Certainly the size and composition of states varies dramatically as well, but states are meaningful political units relative to the federal political system; counties are clearly less so.

Finally, an analysis of military procurement spending is complicated by the process of subcontracting. The first point to make is that the data available at the state level does not report on subcontracting, a point made very well in a General Accounting Office report (GAO/NSIAD-98-139R) on military contracting in New Mexico. However, Rundquist and colleagues (1993) report that most studies find that the majority of subcontracts are distributed to locations near the prime contractor. Furthermore, their study of four major prime contractors' subcontracts finds a strong association between the distribution of subcontracts and the industrial capacity of a place to produce defense-related goods. Given that our analysis presented here controls for industrial capacity, we will have captured some of the subcontracting phenomenon. This work also suggests that much subcontracting work would stay within state borders and the subcontracting that does cross state borders tends to remain in the adjacent states and will be captured by the regional dummy variables we include. For the more limited time series that is available at the district and county levels, researchers can use the Consolidated Annual Federal Reports (CAFR) data that overcome some of the subcontracting problem. An analysis of these data at the district and county levels (see Appendix B) uncovers the same basic findings at all three levels of aggregation. Thus we are confident that using the prime contract data does not significantly affect the validity of our analysis. Whatever subcontracting dispersion of expenditures we fail to capture in our analysis should only bias our analysis against finding significant effects. In other words, whatever slippage there is as a result of failing to capture this portion of expenditures that bleeds across state borders can only lead us to underestimate the relationships among party, committee, and ideological representation, on the one hand, and per capita procurement expenditures, on the other.

In short, there are advantages and disadvantages to conducting this analysis at the state level. We feel the advantages outweigh the disadvantages in this case. States are meaningful political entities that have been shown to structure national political behavior, national policy making generally, the behavior of state delegations in Congress, and defense policy making specifically. Appendix B presents a replication of our basic state-level analysis at the county and district levels. Most of the findings reported here at the state level are also uncovered at the district and county levels. Those that are not replicated generally result from the specific time periods that are available, the sample size available, or the limitations of district- and county-level analysis outlined above.

Data and Measurement

Below we operationalize each variable included in the statistical model presented in table 4.1, noting both the measurement of the variable and the source of data. We have data for every state from 1963 through 1995, giving us 1,650 observations when pooled.[5]

BENEFITS. Our basic measure of defense spending benefits is military procurement spending received by states annually.[6] The variable is measured as the annual dollar amount per capita for each state, adjusted for inflation. These data are taken from the DOD publication *Prime Contract Awards by State and Region, 1959 to 1989*, and from the same source for each year from 1990 through 1995. The mean value for this variable is $337. Thus over the entire period states received, on average, $337 per capita in adjusted (1982–84) dollars in military procurement awards. Of course, not every state received this much in every year. The lowest observed value in our data set is a mere $12 per capita, observed for Montana in 1975 and South Dakota in 1969. In contrast, Connecticut received more than $2,000 per capita in both 1966 and 1968, and Virginia received more that $2,000 per capita in 1995.

COMMITTEE REPRESENTATION. We measure committee representation for each chamber using simple dummy variables. In each instance, if a state has an MC representing it on a House or Senate defense committee for that year, the variable is coded as 1. Otherwise, the variable is coded as 0. When measured as an independent variable, committee representation is split between representation by a Democrat and representation by a Republican. This allows us to test the hypothesis that majority party committee members, as compared to minority party committee members, are better able to retain their seats and to direct benefits back home.

Although we can record the party of a state's representative on the right-hand side of each of the equations in table 4.1 by using two variables, we cannot do so when committee representation serves as a dependent variable. Trying to produce separate estimates of what predicts defense committee representation by Democrats and Republicans in each chamber as part of a set of simultaneous equations would result in a substantial loss of cases. For example, a *dependent* variable measuring whether a state was represented on a Senate defense committee by a Republican in a particular year would have to be coded as missing if a state sent no Republicans to the Senate that year. When estimating the equations simultaneously, that particular case would be dropped from every equation. Considering the number of states that sent one-party delegations to the House and especially to the Senate in various years, the number of cases lost renders the analysis intractable and hopelessly unrepresentative.[7] This is not a problem when measuring committee representation as an independent variable, because a combination of variables can be used to capture all possible combinations of one-party and mixed-party representation in each

equation. Other statistical issues involved with having dichotomous dependent variables as part of a system of equations are discussed in Appendix A.

Data for these measures were taken from the *Congressional Directory* and the *Congressional Quarterly* for each Congress. These
sources were corrected using the *House Journal*, as suggested by
Cox and McCubbins (1993).

PARTY. We measure partisanship directly by recording the percentage of a state's congressional delegation to each chamber that
is Democratic each year. This captures the degree to which a state
is represented in each chamber by what was the majority party for
nearly all of the period under study.[8] As described above, we also
include partisanship in our measures of committee representation
by coding the party of each MC who serves on a defense-related
committee in each chamber. The data for these variables were
taken from the *Congressional Directory* for each Congress.

IDEOLOGY. We measure ideology as the overall (mean) ideological orientation of a state's delegation to the House and the Senate.
We use Conservative Coalition scores prepared by the *Congressional Quarterly* for each year included in our study to construct our
measure of ideology. CC scores indicate the percentage of a wide
range of selected roll call votes on which a majority of southern
Democrats and a majority of Republicans vote together. For example, in 1990 the CC materialized on fifty-four recorded votes, and
the CC score for each member of Congress that year indicates the
percentage of these fifty-four votes on which that member voted
with the CC. The theoretical range of these scores is from 0 to 100,
with higher scores indicating relatively more conservative state
delegations. We use CC scores rather than a measure such as Poole
and Rosenthal's (1997) because of the difficulty in distinguishing
ideology from partisanship in their measure. CC scores are explic-
itly separate from partisanship in that the Conservative Coalition
consists of MCs from both parties.

CAPACITY. In terms of defense spending capacity represents the
ability to translate procurement expenditures into the goods and

services needed to provide for the national defense. More specifically, in the area of defense procurement, capacity represents the ability of a place to build military weapons and equipment. Thus we measure capacity as the level of GSP due to manufacturing per capita in a state, adjusted for inflation. We take this as a surrogate for the relative capacity of a state to manufacture weapons and weapons systems. In addition, Markusen and colleagues (1991) argue that certain areas, located in what they call the Gunbelt, have long been associated with weapons manufacturing. In our view these areas also have a unique capacity to build weapons. As a result, we measure capacity as the per capita GSP due to manufacturing, a dummy variable that measures whether a state is located in the Gunbelt and a multiplicative interaction term between the two. This is the same measurement strategy we employed in other settings (Carsey and Rundquist 1999a, 1999b).

STATE ECONOMIC CONDITIONS. Of course, the entire country is in need of the public good national defense, and in this sense there is no subnational variation in need. However, we are also interested in the role of defense procurement spending in state economic development. We measure the relative health of a state's economy using two variables: state unemployment rate and state per capita income, adjusted for inflation. Those states with relatively higher rates of unemployment and lower per capita incomes could be considered most in need of federal expenditures in the form of military procurement awards. When we examine the impact of military procurement expenditures on state economies, per capita income and unemployment serve as our dependent variables.

The basic model described here allows for comparisons of the empirical validity of several competing distributive hypotheses. It also allows for the analysis of changes in and the accumulation of benefits over time as well as the possibility of interaction between key variables. Finally, it models potential reciprocal relationships that may exist in the distributive politics of defense spending.

CHAPTER FIVE

TARGETING MILITARY PROCUREMENT EXPENDITURES

In this chapter we test the various distributive hypotheses regarding the geographic distribution of military procurement benefits. That is, to what extent are the beneficiaries of year-to-year changes in defense contracting states represented on defense committees, states with delegations of predominantly majority party legislators, states represented by conservative legislators, states with relatively greater economic need for defense procurement expenditures, or states with more economic capacity for doing defense work.

PURE COMMITTEE-BASED TARGETING

The pure committee hypothesis predicts that growth in defense procurement awards will be disproportionately greater in states represented on congressional defense committees. This should be true regardless of whether they are represented by a Democrat or a Republican and regardless of MC ideology. In terms of the statistical model presented in chapter 4, the expectation is that β_2 and β_3 would be positive, statistically significant, and equal to each other in the House and that the same should hold for β_4 and β_5 in the Senate.[1]

As table 5.1 shows, our findings do not support the pure committee benefit hypothesis in either the House or the Senate. It is *not* the case that states represented on defense committees by either Democrats or Republicans tend to benefit equally from military procurement spending. Although it can be shown that House committee representation in general is correlated with defense spending (see Carsey and Rundquist 1999b), most of this effect derives from representation on defense committees by House Democrats. States represented by defense committee Republicans in the House do not benefit. The coefficient of 17.266 reported in table 5.1 means that being represented by a Democrat on a House defense committee in the previous year is worth just over $17.00 per capita in additional military procurement spending the following year. The estimated effect for states represented by Republicans on House defense committees is only an additional $6.07, which is not a statistically significant effect. Thus in the House the pure committee hypothesis does not account for the distribution of military contract awards.

In the Senate the prior committee representation hypothesis receives no support. Table 5.1 reports that the relationship between representation by a Democrat and military procurement awards is actually negative, although it is only weakly significant ($p < .10$). States represented by a Democrat on a Senate committee average $27.30 per capita less than states not represented on defense committees. In contrast, states represented by Republicans average about $14.00 per capita more than states not represented on the committee ($p < .10$). Again, these patterns are characterized by relatively large standard errors, suggesting that the estimated effects of Senate defense committee representation are sufficiently imprecise to be interpreted with caution. The negative finding regarding Senate defense committee Democrats is explored further below, but for now the only conclusion that can be drawn is that in the Senate, just like in the House, there is no evidence of a pure committee representation effect on the distribution of military procurement contracts.

TABLE 5.1.

Factors That Influence the Targeting of Per Capita Military Procurement Spending across the States, 1963–1995

Variable	Unstandardized Coefficient (Standard Error)
Per capita military procurement contracts$_{t-1}$	.811(.031)***
House Democrat on defense committee$_{t-1}$	17.266(5.677)***
House Republican on defense committee$_{t-1}$	6.067(7.117)
Senate Democrat on defense committee$_{t-1}$	-27.290(14.591)*
Senate Republican on defense committee$_{t-1}$	14.032(7.927)*
Percentage of Democrats in House delegation$_t$	-.088(.136)
Percentage of Democrats in Senate delegation$_t$	-.039(.099)
House delegation ideology$_{t-1}$	-.228(.238)
Senate delegation ideology$_{t-1}$	-.469(.176)***
Senate Democrat on defense committee x Senate delegation ideology$_{t-1}$	.813(.270)**
Per capita GSP due to manufacturing$_{t-1}$	-.003(.004)
Gunbelt state	-4.027(20.959)
Per capita GSP x Gunbelt state$_{t-1}$	.021(.009)**
Per capita income$_{t-1}$	.009(.003)***
Percentage unemployed$_{t-1}$	1.171(1.755)
R-squared	.86

NOTE: N = 1,600. Robust standard errors computed as suggested by Beck and Katz (1995). Estimates produced are part of a full model of Seemingly Unrelated Regression equations. Results from the other equations are reported in subsequent chapters. This equation also includes a set of dummy variables to control for region and year.

*p < .1, **p < .05, ***p < .01.

PURE PARTY-BASED TARGETING

There is no evidence of a pure party effect on the distribution of military contracts. The hypothesis is that the larger the percentage of a state's House or Senate delegations that belong to the majority party,[2] the more military procurement dollars per capita it should receive. Moreover, this effect should occur independently of any impact of committee representation or ideology. Table 5.1 reveals no empirical support for this hypothesis. The coefficient operating on the House party variable is −.088, and the coefficient for the Senate party variable is −.039. Neither coefficient even approaches statistical significance. We have already seen that states represented by Democrats on House defense committees receive additional defense procurement awards. Thus the only evidence of a partisan impact on the distribution of procurement expenditures is one that is contingent on defense committee representation.

PURE IDEOLOGY-BASED TARGETING

There is no support for a pure ideology effect on the distribution of defense procurement spending. The hypothesis here is that states represented by more conservative delegations in the House or Senate will receive disproportionately larger increases in military procurement benefits. Table 5.1 shows that states represented by more conservative delegations in the House do not receive additional benefits. The coefficient estimate is actually negative (−.228) but does not approach statistical significance.

The findings are more mixed in the Senate. There is no pure ideology effect. Thus in models that test only for the direct effect of Senate ideology, we find no significant relationship between ideology and the distribution of military procurement benefits. However, if we interact ideology with defense committee representation, the pattern changes. As table 5.1 shows, states with relatively more conservative state delegations in the Senate receive significantly fewer defense procurement dollars per capita ($\beta = -.469, p < .01$). For every increase of 1 point in Senate ideology (becoming more conservative on a 1 to 100 scale), the per capita procurement contract awards received by a state in the following year declines by $0.47.

However, we also find a significant tendency for states to benefit if their Senate delegation is composed of conservatives *and* they are represented on a Senate defense committee by a Democrat. The relevant coefficient reported in table 5.1 that captures this effect is .813 ($p < .05$). This means that for those states represented by a Democrat on a Senate defense committee, an increase in their Senate delegation ideology score of 1 point results in an increase in per capita military procurement awards of $0.81. Figure 5.1 illustrates this interactive effect. If a state is represented by a liberal Senate delegation, such that its mean CC score is below 33, and it has a Democratic member on a Senate defense committee, it tends to receive less in military procurement spending. However, if a state has a Democratic senator on a defense committee *and* its Senate delegation is relatively conservative, it receives significantly more military procurement expenditures.

There is a regional pattern in the ideological orientation of Democratic senators, as conservative Democrats come predominantly from the South. However, the patterns reported here are not simply artifacts of regional differences in the distribution of military contracts, because the analysis includes a set of eight regional dummy variables. Thus the positive impact of being represented by a conservative Democrat on a Senate defense committee operates independently of regional patterns in the distribution of defense spending.

INTRAPOLICY UNIVERSALISM

Intrapolicy universalism predicts that states with an interest in receiving military procurement benefits will in fact receive them. Separating "interest" from other factors such as committee representation, party, or ideology is difficult, and our models do not include a specific variable that captures interest. However, one

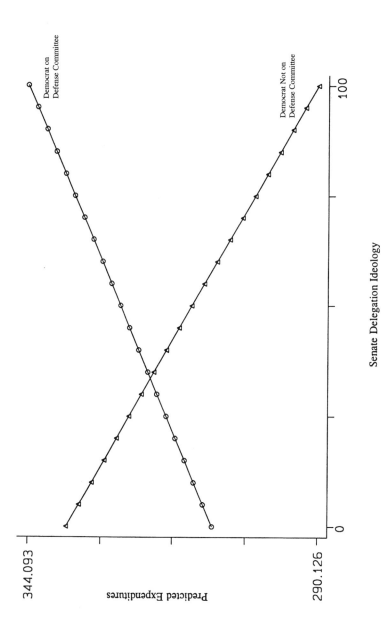

Fig. 5.1. Predicted per capita military procurement expenditures as a function of Senate defense committee representation by a Democrat and State Senate delegation ideology, 1963–1995.

measure of interest might be the previous level of defense procurement expenditures received by a state. Table 5.1 shows a significant effect ($.811, p < .01$) of the previous year's benefit level on the current year's. This is not surprising. To take this effect as evidence of intrapolicy universalism would no doubt overestimate the presence of this effect, because other unmeasured factors certainly contribute to the autoregressiveness of the geographic distribution of military procurement spending. However, we have controlled for a number of relevant factors, including the effects of party, ideology, committee representation, industrial capacity, and economic conditions, along with the region and year dummy variables. So we believe that at least part of the remaining autoregressive effect can be attributed to constituency interest in continued receipt of defense procurement expenditures.

Of course, that all the other factors described thus far also influence year-to-year changes in the geographic distribution of benefits runs counter to the *pure* intrapolicy universalism prediction that only constituency interest should be at work. Thus to the extent that intrapolicy universalism is operative, it is contingent on the operation of these other factors. Conversely, one might want to argue that these other variables cause short-term deviations from what pure intrapolicy universalism would predict.

INTERPOLICY UNIVERSALISM

Evaluating the version of universalism that predicts vote trading across policy areas in a study that looks at only one policy area may seem to stretch beyond the limits of the analysis. However, the traditional theory of interpolicy universalism (Shepsle and Weingast 1981, 1995) that focuses on the so-called gains from exchange leads to the prediction that the beneficiaries of any particular policy area (such as defense) should be places represented on the relevant congressional committees. We have already shown that the pure committee-based theory does not hold in the case of military procurement expenditures. Therefore, our evidence is also inconsistent with the interpolicy universalism version of distributive theory. Of course, interpolicy logrolling could take place in a manner that is structured by the more complex set of party, committee, and ideology effects we have uncovered regarding defense procurement spending. If so, a more complicated theory of interpolicy universalism might be supported.

ECONOMIC CONDITION-BASED TARGETING

Are military procurement expenditures targeted at states with higher levels of joblessness or lower per capita incomes, or do they target relatively wealthy states? Our findings based on the entire 1963 through 1995 period suggests two things. First, table 5.1 shows that there is no tendency for states with higher levels of unemployment to benefit more from military procurement spending. The coefficient is positive (1.171) but does not approach statistical significance. Chapter 9 shows that for some short periods this is not the case. But for the whole period, we find no support for the hypothesis that military procurement expenditures have targeted states with higher rates of joblessness.

We do find a relationship between change in the distribution of military procurement expenditures and state per capita income. However, the relationship reported in table 5.1 is positive rather than negative. Additional per capita military procurement expenditures are targeted to states with *higher* levels of per capita income. The coefficient of .009 ($p < .01$) means that increases in state per capita income of $100 would result in a state receiving an additional $0.90 per capita in military procurement spending. Thus the targeting that occurs appears to benefit states that have relatively wealthier populations over those with lower average incomes. Russett (1970) argues that the geographic distribution of military spending results in wealthier places getting even wealthier. In chapter 9 we explore the economic impact of defense procurement awards on state economies. But for now, we see evidence supporting at least the first half of Russett's claim: relatively wealthier states receive disproportionately larger increases in military procurement expenditures.

CAPACITY-BASED TARGETING

A primary objective of military procurement spending is the production of goods that provide for the national defense. To do this effectively, military procurement expenditures should target places most able to produce military goods and services. We measure capacity as per capita GSP due to manufacturing. We also compare Gunbelt states with other states. Table 5.1 shows that we uncovered no evidence that simply being a Gunbelt state resulted in receiving disproportionately higher levels of procurement awards, as the coefficient (–4.027) was only one-fourth the size of its standard error (20.959). Similarly, we find no direct effect of per capita GSP due to manufacturing on changes in military procurement expenditures. However, we do find an interactive effect of these two variables by which states benefit more from changes in the distribution of miliary procurement expenditures. Table 5.1 shows that Gunbelt states were advantaged only when they also evidenced relatively greater capacity to translate procurement awards into the products deemed necessary for the national defense. The coefficient of .021 ($p < .05$) means that when per capita GSP due to manufacturing increases in Gunbelt states by \$100, the level of per capita military procurement contracts received increases by about \$2.

A HYBRID MODEL OF THE DISTRIBUTIVE POLITICS OF DEFENSE PROCUREMENT

The findings presented in this chapter make it clear that the impact of political factors on the distribution of military procurement awards cannot be narrowly understood as *purely* committee based, party based, or ideology based. Nor is it the case that intrapolicy or interpolicy universalism alone can account for the distribution of defense procurement benefits. Rather our findings suggest that elements of each of these views of distributive politics combine to shape the distribution of military procurement expenditures, and they do so differently in the House and the Senate. In the House the targeting of year-to-year changes in the distribution of military procurement expenditures is conditioned by the interaction between committee representation and representation by majority party members. Cox and McCubbins (1993) and Shepsle and Weingast (1995) suggest that such a party-committee hybrid model might resolve some of the disagreements among congressional scholars regarding distributive policy making.

In the Senate it is the interaction among committee representation, party, and the ideology of the state delegation that is reflected in the distribution of year-to-year changes in the distribution of military procurement expenditures. States that send conservative delegations to the Senate and also are represented on Senate defense committees by conservative Democrats benefit most. Compared to the House, then, it is a more narrowly defined set of senators that successfully secures additional military procurement benefits for their states. Liberal Democrats on defense committees are unable to secure additional benefits. In both chambers we see an influence of being represented on a defense committee. In the House it is all defense committee Democrats whose states are targeted. In the Senate it is only conservative Democrats on defense committees whose states are targeted for benefits.

Our findings contradict the *intra*policy universalism hypothesis that all or nearly all states with an interest in receiving military procurement expenditures should benefit to the exclusion of other factors. Clearly, states represented on defense committees by Republicans and states not represented on defense committees at all are *not* targeted for benefits. However, the evidence of targeting based on capacity and the strong influence that the previous year's distribution has on the subsequent year's distribution is consistent with the existence of an *intra*policy universalism norm. Similarly, *inter*policy universalism as it relates to predictions of logrolling across policy areas is *not* supported because Republican committee members do not benefit. Our findings do not preclude the existence of logrolling, but the general assumption that interpolicy universalism occurs primarily in line with the committee structure of Congress is too simplistic to capture any intercommittee vote trading that might involve military procurement expenditures. If interpolicy logrolling does take place, our findings suggest that it is among majority party members on different committees.

Finally, we find evidence that relatively wealthier states received disproportionately larger increases in defense procurement funds. This conflicts with the view that defense procurement expenditures might be targeted to economically poor states.

Our analysis of a set of competing hypotheses about political factors that might directly influence the distribution of military procurement contracts shows that year-to-year changes in the distribution of military procurement spending respond to a fairly complex combination of these factors. In the House we find that the effects of party and committee representation interact to positively influence the distribution of defense procurement contracts. This finding is consistent with the argument that the majority party in the House is able to use the committee system to further the interests of its members. In the Senate we see evidence that this effect is further conditioned by the ideological orientation of a state's Senate delegation, so that only states represented on Senate defense committees by conservative Democrats are so targeted. There is also evidence of interest-based targeting as predicted by intrapolicy universalism.

CHAPTER SIX

COMMITTEE REPRESENTATION

The logic of the committee representation hypothesis in distributive theories follows directly from that of the benefit targeting hypotheses explored in chapter 5. The committee representation hypothesis posits that because there are benefits to be had, MCs who want to bring these benefits to their states will seek membership on defense committees. Intrapolicy universalism suggests the opposite. Because members who want to bring military procurement benefits to their state can do so regardless of whether they are on a defense committee, there is no need for them to become committee members. In this chapter we explore these ideas in both the House and the Senate. We also consider the relative importance of party, ideology, need, and capacity in predicting defense committee representation in each chamber.

The first hypothesis we examine is that states that receive more defense contracts per capita in one year are more likely to be represented on a defense committee in the following year. In testing this hypothesis, we estimate separate equations for the House and the Senate. The dependent variable for each equation is a dummy variable, coded 1 if the state is represented on a House (Senate) defense committee or a defense subcommittee of the Appropriations Committee and 0 otherwise. Chapter 4 and Appendix A discuss the methodological issues related to this analysis.[1] Recall that our model controls for whether the state was represented in the previous year, which means that here we are considering the impact of last year's level of military procurement awards on *changes* in the probability of a state being represented on a defense committee from last year to this year.

Table 6.1 shows that we find support for the committee recruitment hypothesis in both the House and the Senate. Previous levels of per capita defense contracts have a positive and significant effect on the probability that a state will be represented on a House defense committee. The coefficient reported in the first column of table 6.1 is small (.00018) but clearly significant ($p < .01$). The coefficient means that for every increase in per capita defense contracts of $300 (about one standard deviation) in one year, the probability that a state will be represented on a House defense committee the next year increases by about 5.5 percentage points. For the Senate, the estimated effect reported in the second column of table 6.1 is smaller (.000074) but still significant ($p < .05$). Every increase in per capita defense contract awards of $300 (one standard deviation) increases the probability of a state being represented on a Senate defense committee in the subsequent year by 2.2 percentage points. Thus MCs from states that receive higher levels of military procurement awards do appear more likely to obtain a seat on a defense committee. This suggests that defense committee seats are seen as valuable by MCs from states with high levels of defense contracting. These MCs may view defense committee seats as useful in protecting the level of benefits already received by a state and as enabling them to direct additional benefits to their states. This of course contradicts the intrapolicy universalism view that all states with an interest in receiving military procurement benefits should get them regardless of whether they are represented on a defense committee.

PARTY EFFECTS

Hypotheses regarding the influence of partisanship on defense committee representation take two forms. The first, which parallels

TABLE 6.1.

Factors that Influence the Probability That a State Is Represented on a House or Senate Defense Committee, 1963–1995

Variable	House	Senate
Per capita military procurement contracts$_{t-1}$	.00018(.00003)***	.000074(.000036)**
Democrat on defense committee$_{t-1}$	.687(.052)***	.934(.040)***
Republican on a defense committee$_{t-1}$	.138(.069)**	.685(.055)***
Percentage of Democrats in chamber delegation$_{t-1}$	.0002(.0002)	.001(.0002)***
Chamber delegation ideology$_{t-1}$	.0017(.0005)***	.0035(.0005)***
Democrat on defense committee × chamber delegation ideology$_{t-1}$	-.0022(.0008)***	-.0043(.00065)***
Republican on defense committee × chamber delegation ideology$_{t-1}$	.0035(.0011)***	-.0009(.0008)
Per capita GSP due to manufacturing$_{t-1}$	.00003(.000008)***	-.000028(.000012)**
Gunbelt state	.143(.038)***	-.0099(.047)
Per capita GSP x Gunbelt state$_{t-1}$	-.000073(.00002)***	.00007(.00002)
Per capita income$_{t-1}$	-.000001(.000004)	.0000057(.0000033)*
Percentage unemployed$_{t-1}$	-.005(.0025)**	-.0007(.003)
Size of House delegation (logged)	.051(.011)***	----
R-squared	.72	.67
Percent of cases correctly predicted	94	91

NOTE: $N = 1,600$. Robust standard errors computed as suggested by Beck and Katz (1995). Estimates produced are part of a full model of Seemingly Unrelated Regression equations. Results from the other equations are reported in subsequent chapters. This equation also includes a set of dummy variables to control for region and year.

*$p < .1$, **$p < .05$, ***$p < .01$.

the pure party hypothesis regarding benefits, suggests that states sending predominantly majority party (in our case, Democratic) delegations to the House and Senate will be more likely to obtain representation on a defense committee. This hypothesis follows from the argument that the majority party structures policy making in Congress and that one way it does so is to use the committee structure to benefit members of the majority party.

The second hypothesis is related to the first. If the majority party assigns members to defense committees in order to enhance their reelection chances or to allow them to focus on policy problems of greater interest to them, we would expect to see that states already represented on a defense committee by a majority party member would be more likely to retain that representation than states already represented on a defense committee by a minority party member.

The first column of table 6.1 reports no evidence that states represented by House delegations made up largely of majority party members are any more likely to obtain representation on a House defense committee than states with delegations composed mostly of minority party members. The coefficient is very close to 0 (.0002), and it does not approach statistical significance.

In contrast, we find a positive and significant relationship between increases in the number of Democratic senators from a state and obtaining representation on a Senate defense committee. The coefficient of .001 reported in the second column of table 6.1 means that a state with two Democrats in the Senate has a probability of being represented on a Senate defense committee that is about 10 percentage points higher than that of a state with two Republicans in the Senate. Taken together, these findings show no evidence of a pure party effect on defense committee representation in the House, but there is some evidence of such an effect in the Senate.

Our second hypothesis regarding partisanship is that states represented by defense committee members from the majority party will be more likely to retain their defense committee representation than will states represented by defense committee members from the minority party. The evidence for both the House and the Senate reported in table 6.1 confirms this prediction. Regardless of party, states represented on defense committees in the previous year have a higher probability of being represented on defense committees the following year than do states that were not represented on a defense committee in the previous year. However, this effect is much larger for states represented by Democrats on the defense committees than for states represented by Republicans. The coefficient for previous House defense committee representation by a Democrat is .687, while the coefficient for Republicans in the House is .138. The two coefficients for previous defense committee representation in the Senate are .934 for Democrats and .685 for Republicans. In both chambers the difference between the Democratic and Republican coefficients is statistically significant.[2]

IDEOLOGY EFFECTS

Are states with relatively more conservative delegations in Congress more likely to gain representation on a defense committee in either the House or the Senate? Scholars have struggled with the nature of the relationship between MC ideology and their behavior (e.g., Shepsle 1978; Lindsay 1990; Krehbiel 1991; Jackson and Kingdon 1992). One difficulty with such analyses is separating the influence of MC ideology from that of the economic interests of each member's constituency (Kao and Rubin 1982). The question is whether MCs support (or oppose) defense spending and/or seek (or do not seek) membership on defense committees because their own ideology tends to be hawkish (or dovish) or because their behavior regarding defense spending and defense committee representation simply reflects their constituency's economic interests.[3] We cannot provide a complete solution to this puzzle here, but we offer two points.

First, recall that the portion of our model that predicts committee representation controls for previous levels of military procurement contracts. If previous level of military contracts captures a state's economic interest in receiving military procurement awards, then any effect we find of delegation ideology should reveal true ideological effects.[4]

Second, if our measure of delegation ideology reflected only the state's economic interest in military procurement contracts, then one would expect that changes in the ideological orientation of a state's delegation would respond to the level of procurement awards a state receives. In other words, one might expect a reciprocal relationship between the geographic distribution of military procurement expenditures and delegation ideology. However, our analysis (not shown here) finds that previous benefit levels are not related to the subsequent ideological makeup of the delegations states send to either the House or the Senate. This suggests that our measure of MC ideology captures something other than pure economic interest in acquiring or protecting benefits.

The analysis reported in table 6.1 shows that states that send more conservative delegations to either the House or the Senate increase their chances of gaining representation on defense committees. In the House, comparing the most liberal to the most conservative state delegation, we observe an increase in the probability of being represented on a defense committee of about 17 percentage points. In the Senate, the effect is larger. The probability of the most conservative state delegation being represented on a Senate defense committee is 35 percentage points higher than that for states represented by the most liberal delegation. This is clear evidence that states with more conservative delegations tend to be overrepresented on defense committees and that the effect of ideology is independent of other factors, including the previous level of military procurement expenditures targeted to a state.

However, the effects of ideology on changes in the probability of a state being represented on a congressional defense committee depend on whether a state was previously represented on a defense committee, and if so, by which party. In the House, the positive effect of ideology on defense committee representation becomes slightly negative for states already represented on a defense committee in the previous year by a Democrat. The rather large direct effect of being represented by a Democrat reported above, however, more than outweighs this slight negative interactive effect between ideology and previous representation by a Democrat. As figure 6.1 illustrates, being represented in the previous year by a Democrat on a House defense committee, regardless of ideology, has a greater impact on the probability of a state's subsequent defense committee representation than does its delegation's ideology.

In contrast, figure 6.1 shows that the effect of ideology on subsequent committee representation is intensified if a state was previously represented on a House defense committee by a Republican. Thus the direct effect of ideology on defense committee representation ranging across the ideological scale (reported above as being about 17 percentage points) increases to about 51 percentage points if the state was also previously represented by a Republican on a defense committee. In other words, the combined effect of having a conservative state delegation and being previously represented on a defense committee by a Republican is about the same as being previously represented by a Democrat regardless of ideological stripe.

To summarize, we find evidence of an ideological effect on defense committee representation. There is a pure ideology effect in the Senate but an ideological effect conditioned by partisanship and previous defense committee representation in the House.

ECONOMIC CONDITION EFFECTS

Here we consider whether either of our measures of economic need—low levels of per capita income and high state unemployment rates—predict subsequent representation for a state on a defense committee in either the House or the Senate. The results in table 6.1 show that there is no statistically significant effect of per capita income on whether a state is represented on a defense committee in the House. We find a statistically significant, though negative, effect of state unemployment on changes in the probability of being represented on a House defense committee. States with higher

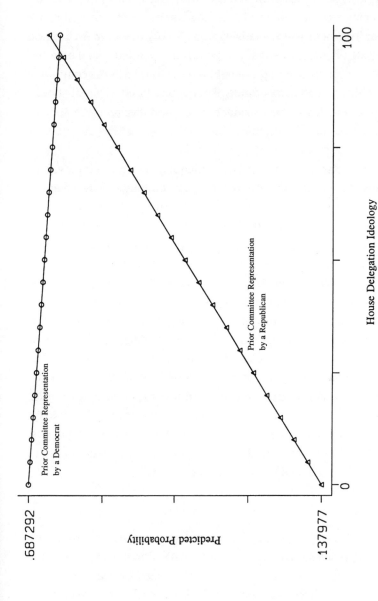

Fig. 6.1. Predicted probability of House defense committee representation as a function of prior House defense committee representation and House delegation ideology, 1963–1995.

levels of unemployment in a given year have a lower probability of being represented on a House defense committee the following year. The coefficient is relatively small (–.005), however. An increase in state unemployment of one percentage point lowers the probability of subsequent representation on a House defense committee by only one-half of a percentage point, but the effect is statistically significant. Thus we see evidence that committee representation in the House may, if anything, impede somewhat the targeting of benefits to poorer states.

In the Senate we do not find evidence that state unemployment rates are significantly related to defense committee representation. However, we find a statistically significant positive relationship between state per capita income and Senate defense committee representation. States with higher per capita incomes are more likely to obtain representation on a Senate defense committee than are states with lower per capita incomes. The effect appears relatively small, with an increase in state per capita income of $2,500 (about one standard deviation) resulting in an increased probability of a state being represented on a Senate defense committee of about 1.5 percentage points. However, the conclusion remains that representation on a Senate defense committee interferes with targeting military procurement expenditures to poorer states. Earlier we noted that military procurement benefits are more likely to go to states with higher per capita incomes. Our findings here suggest that wealthier states are also slightly more likely than poor ones to be represented on defense committees as well.

CAPACITY EFFECTS

Are states with more capacity for defense contracting more likely to obtain defense committee representation? In the previous chapter we found that military procurement benefits targeted places of relatively higher capacity, at least in the Gunbelt. Here we find that defense committee representation also responds to capacity, although in a slightly different way. First, we see a direct effect of higher levels of capacity on representation on a House defense committee for those states outside the Gunbelt. For every increase in per capita GSP due to manufacturing of one standard deviation (about $1,161) outside the Gunbelt, a state increases its probability of being represented on a House defense committee by about 3.5 percentage points.

Second, we see a direct effect on House defense committee representation for states in the Gunbelt. Specifically, Gunbelt states are about 14 percentage points more likely to gain representation on a House defense committee than are their non-Gunbelt counterparts. In a somewhat surprising finding, however, as capacity increases in the Gunbelt, the probability of a state gaining representation on a House defense committee decreases. The effect of a one standard deviation increase in capacity within the Gunbelt on the probability of gaining defense committee representation is to lower it by almost 5 percentage points. The net result is that Gunbelt states of relatively low capacity are more likely to gain representation on a House defense committee than are low-capacity states outside the Gunbelt. However, as state capacity approaches the mean for the 1963–95 period of about $2,500, the advantage Gunbelt states had in obtaining defense committee representation is eliminated, such that among states with relatively higher capacities, those outside the Gunbelt are more likely to gain representation on a House defense committee. This relationship is illustrated in figure 6.2, which for ease of presentation assumes a base probability of being represented on a House defense committee of .5. This is a point to which we return below.

The effect of capacity on defense committee representation in the Senate is more limited. The only impact on Senate defense committee representation occurs outside the Gunbelt, and, oddly, the effect is negative. States outside the Gunbelt with higher per capita GSP due to manufacturing are less likely to gain a seat on a Senate defense committee. The effect is fairly small, however, with an increase in capacity of one standard deviation leading to a reduced probability of being represented on a Senate defense committee of about 3.2 percentage points.

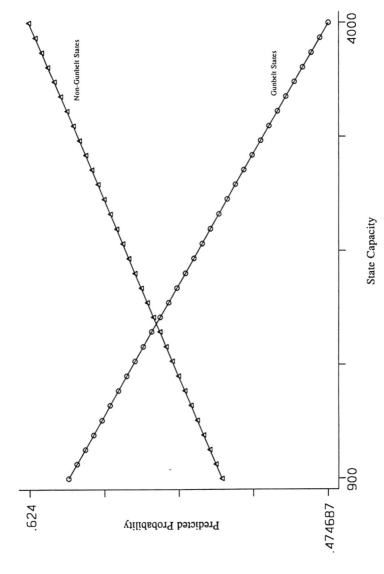

Fig. 6.2. Predicted probability of House defense committee representation as a function of state industrial capacity for Gunbelt and Non-Gunbelt states, 1963–1995.

In chapter 5 we saw that military procurement awards are targeted to states in the Gunbelt with relatively larger capacities. Here we see that Gunbelt states are also more likely to be represented on House defense committees. Yet, as we have just shown, states outside the Gunbelt that have relatively higher capacities are also more likely to gain representation on a House defense committee. This suggests that, at least in the House, the committee representation process fosters the targeting of additional funds to high-capacity non-Gunbelt states. It does so because these states are more likely to gain House defense committee representation, and as Chapter 5 shows, House defense committee representation results in additional procurement expenditures being directed toward a state.

We have provided additional evidence that the distributive politics of military procurement spending is structured by majority party status, prior committee representation, and local interest in military contracting. Members of the majority party are better able than members of the minority party to retain defense committee representation. We have found strong evidence that previous receipt of military contracts results in subsequent representation on defense committees. And we have seen that states with more conservative congressional delegations are more likely to obtain representation on defense committees. Our findings regarding the effect of capacity and state economic conditions are mixed.

Our analysis of defense committee representation suggests support for the party-, committee-, and ideology-centered versions of distributive theory. It is also consistent with interpolicy universalism, because MCs from states that have a strong interest in defense contracting (i.e., have been receiving defense contracts) tend to get new assignments on defense committees. Finally, we have found limited evidence of a pure committee effect in that states represented on a defense committee are likely to retain that representation. Although this is true of committee members from both parties, the retention effect is significantly stronger for majority party members on the committees.

CHAPTER SEVEN

CUMULATIVE EFFECTS AND OVERALL FIT

CUMULATIVE EFFECTS

To this point we have considered our findings only in terms of a one-year impact on defense benefits or committee representation. For example, we reported in chapter 5 that states represented on a House defense committee by a Democrat in one year receive about $17 in additional per capita procurement awards in the following year. Yet this onetime impact captures only part of the picture.

We have shown that the geographic distribution of per capita military procurement awards exhibits a fairly strong autoregressive process, meaning that the distribution of military procurement benefits that exists in one year strongly influences the distribution of benefits in subsequent years. Once something affects the amount of procurement awards received by a state in a particular year, that onetime bump will continue to be felt in subsequent years. To illustrate, while House defense committee representation by a Democrat in the previous year produces on average $17.00 more in procurement awards per capita in the next year, that additional $17.00 in turn produces another $13.80 the year after that and $9.07 the year after that. These subsequent year effects result from our estimate (in chap. 5) of a coefficient of .811 linking current levels of procurement awards to the previous year's level. For every dollar per capita of military procurement benefits received by a state in a given year, the model predicts that it will receive 81 cents the following year.

If a state is represented for just one year on a House defense committee by a Democrat, our model predicts that is worth about $17 per capita in the next year but a total of almost $79 per capita over a ten-year period. Furthermore, if the state is represented *continuously* on a House defense committee by a Democrat for ten years, at the end of that period the state will have received an increase in per capita military procurement awards of $561.[1]

Cumulative effects characterize all of the variables that were found in chapter 5 to be statistically significant predictors of changes in military procurement expenditures. Similar cumulative effects also characterize the committee representation process described in chapter 6 and the impact of procurement benefits on economic growth we report in chapter 9, because all of these processes are strongly autoregressive. Rather than work through a number of additional examples, we discuss the broader implications that this sort of analysis illustrates.

Both short-term and long-term benefits are available to MCs, benefits that can become quite substantial over their careers. This steady building of military procurement benefits results from committee representation and the steady growth in the probability of gaining additional committee representation. This may shed some light on both the reelection rates of incumbent MCs and the stability of the seniority system in congressional committee assignments. Because incumbents are able to direct a steady and, all things equal, steadily increasing stream of benefits back to their states, they can insulate themselves from electoral challenge (Bickers and Stein, 1996; Levitt and Snyder 1997). Moreover, increasing military procurement benefit levels provide an incentive for voters to retain their representation on defense committees. Thus MCs may choose to protect, sustain, and expand existing military procurement benefits rather than risk switching committees in an effort to tap new benefit pools in different policy areas. The decision to seek defense committee representation or retain it is reinforced by the fact that income growth takes place in states as the result of receiving increased military procurement expenditures (see chap. 9). Income growth in a state is tied to increased defense procurement dollars, but the reverse is also true: a decline in per capita defense procurement awards is associated with declining per capita incomes in a state. Defense committee members able to initiate and expand a benefit stream of defense procurement awards would have little incentive to switch committees, and constituents in states represented on defense committees would have little incentive (all things being equal) to remove those MCs from office.

OVERALL FIT: FORECASTING THE DISTRIBUTION IN 1995

In evaluating the overall fit of the statistical model we estimated for this analysis, we consider the ability of the model to fit the data for the entire 1963–95 period as well as to predict the geographic distribution of military procurement awards and defense committee representation in the final year of our study. The first approach is fairly standard and will be dealt with relatively briefly. The latter, on which we focus more attention, essentially amounts to using our statistical estimates to forecast the values of the dependent variables for the final year of the study and then comparing those predicted values to the actual data for 1995.[2] This will provide an indication of the model's ability to account for the changes observed in the distribution of these variables from 1963 to 1995.

For the entire 1963–95 period, the correlation between per capita military procurement contracts and the predicted value of such awards generated by the statistical model is .93. Expressed differently, the bottom of table 5.1 notes that the R-square for the benefits equation was .86, indicating that 86 percent of the variance in per capita military contracts distributed across the states for the entire 1963–95 period is accounted for by the statistical model. Compared to the 17 percent variance in the 1995 distribution of defense procurement contracts that can be accounted for by knowing the distribution in 1965 (see chap. 1), our estimates make a substantial contribution to explaining how the geographic distribution of procurement benefits in the early 1960s became the distribution that we observe in 1995. Note also that, even with a fairly large coefficient operating on the lagged value of per capita contracts (β = .811), tracing the indirect effect of the existing distribution of benefits in 1965 on the ultimate distribution in 1995 that works through this autoregressive parameter, one would find that the effect is .0018. In other words, a change of $1.00 in per capita procurement benefits in 1965 can be said to produce a change of only $0.0018, or less than two-tenths of a cent, in the 1995 distribution. Another way of saying this is that only about .2 percent of the predicted effect of the distribution of procurement benefits in 1994 on the same distribution in 1995 results from the indirect effect of 1965's distribution working through the autoregressive process. Clearly, our model and statistical estimates capture a large degree of the variation in per capita contracts over the time period in question.

The simple bivariate correlation between the values predicted by our analysis and the actual values of per capita military procurement contracts for the 1995 data is only .79. However, dropping Virginia, an obvious outlier,[3] raises the correlation to an impressive .95. Thus it appears that, except for Virginia, our estimates of the factors that influence the year-to-year changes in the geographic distribution of military procurement awards are also able to account for the level of military procurement spending in each state in 1995. The fit of the model for 1995 is illustrated in figures 7.1 and 7.2.

Figure 7.1 plots the actual versus the predicted values for per capita military procurement spending for all states but Virginia for 1995. The line running through the graph represents the expected location of each state if the statistical model predicted the level of military procurement contracts awarded to states perfectly. Figure 7.1 reveals how tightly the states cluster along the predicted line. This illustrates the ability of the model to correctly predict the geographic distribution of procurement awards for 1995. The statistical model predicts the level of expenditures in states that receive

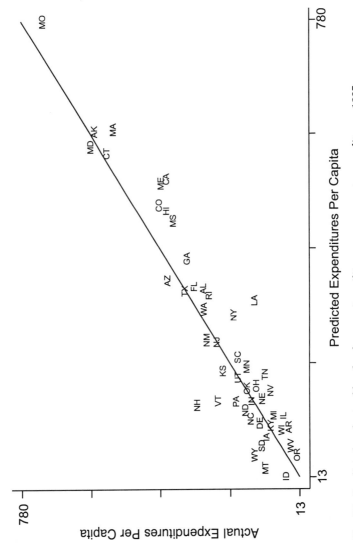

Fig. 7.1. Predicted and actual levels of per capita military procurement expenditures, 1995.

relatively lower levels of military procurement expenditures about as well as it predicts the level for states that receive the most in per capita procurement awards.

Figure 7.2 presents two maps. The first map shows the geographic distribution of actual defense procurement awards for 1995 that we presented in chapter 1. The second map shows the level of per capita procurement awards across states for 1995 predicted by our analysis. The same cut points for the four quartiles used to produce the first map and all those presented in chapter 1 are also used to divide the predicted values into four quartiles in the maps in figure 7.2. While several states shift slightly to neighboring quartiles, the overall impression is that our analysis captures the basic geographic distribution of defense procurement awards in 1995. The same states that are predicted to receive relatively higher levels of per capita defense procurement contracts (the darker shaded states) are in fact those that did.

The estimates from the statistical model also accurately predict defense committee representation. The bottom of table 6.1 reported that for the entire time period, the analysis accounts for 72 percent of the variance in defense committee representation in the House and 67 percent in the Senate. These values are lower than the 86 percent figure for per capita procurement contracts probably because of the dichotomous nature of the two committee representation dependent variables. A more common method of evaluating a model's fit when the dependent variable is dichotomous is to report on the percentage of the cases that are correctly predicted. At the bottom of table 6.1, we see that our estimates correctly predict 1,545 of the 1,650 (94%) state-year cases for House committee representation for the entire time period. In the Senate we correctly predict 1,504 of the 1,650 (91%) cases. Focusing specifically on 1995, our model correctly predicts whether a state is represented on a House defense committee in forty-three of the fifty (86%) states. The model correctly predicts defense committee representation for forty-six of the fifty (92%) states in the Senate for 1995.

Actual Expenditures

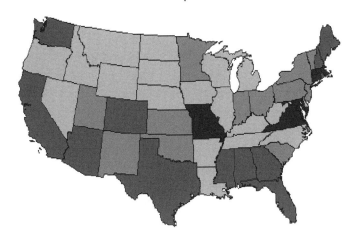

Predicted Expenditures

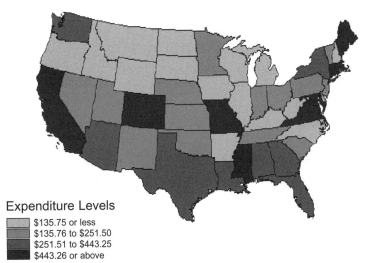

Expenditure Levels

- $135.75 or less
- $135.76 to $251.50
- $251.51 to $443.25
- $443.26 or above

Fig. 7.2. Actual and predicted levels of per capita military procurement expenditures, 1995.

A substantial amount of variation in the distribution of per capita defense procurement contracts, as well as defense committee representation in both chambers of Congress, can be accounted for by our statistical model. The model fits the data for the entire period well, but it also does a good job of predicting the resulting distribution of defense committee representation and military procurement expenditures in 1995, the final year included in our study. Much has happened between 1965 and 1995 to influence the distribution of defense procurement contracts across the states, including the Vietnam war, the Reagan buildup, and the end of the cold war. Much of the change has been incremental from one year to the next, but all of this ultimately results in a distribution of military procurement expenditures in 1995 that differs substantially from the distribution observed thirty years earlier. This chapter shows that our analytic model, which includes several distributive politics variables, explains much of the variation in military procurement expenditures during the thirty-two years of our study.

CHAPTER EIGHT

TRENDS IN THE DISTRIBUTIVE POLITICS OF MILITARY PROCUREMENT SPENDING, 1963–1995

Thus far we have focused on the average influence of each independent variable on changes in the distribution of military procurement expenditures and defense committee representation. Here we explore whether the parameter estimates themselves vary over time. We have seen that the distribution of military procurement awards and defense committee representation in the House are reciprocally related, but is that relationship steady over the entire 1963–95 period? We have seen an interplay among committee, party, and ideological effects on the distribution of military procurement awards, but is the relative influence of each factor steady over time? If not, does an increased effect of one factor necessarily lead to a decreased effect of another? These are the sorts of questions we consider in this chapter. We do not explore whether the basic structure of our analytic model of distributive politics changes but whether the relative effects of committee, party, and ideology on the geographic distribution of military procurement spending and defense committee representation change over time. In the language of statistics, we are not changing the structure of the equations to be estimated, just allowing for the parameter estimates to vary over time.

The analysis in this chapter is exploratory in nature. Our first objective is to examine whether the parameter estimates reported in chapters 5 and 6 change, and if so, to simply describe how they change. Our second objective is to make a preliminary attempt to explain the changes we observe. To guide this exploration, we consider three hypotheses. The first we label the "distributive moments" hypothesis, which draws loosely on Krehbiel's (1998) theory of pivotal politics. Krehbiel argues that policy making, defined as adopting legislation that deviates from the status quo, is facilitated when an election (typically presidential) produces a substantial shift in the agenda pursued by the president and a super-majority in Congress that favors a change in policy over the status quo. Expressed in terms of distributive politics, changing the status quo policy means changing the distribution of policy benefits and committee representation. Here we consider whether distributive moments occur and whether the periods following them are characterized by a different pattern of relationships among our variables.

The second hypothesis we call the "instrumental" hypothesis. Applied to defense procurement, the instrumental hypothesis predicts that leading policy makers (e.g., the president or the bureaucracy), in pursuit of other policy objectives, use military procurement benefits as a means to pursue those other objectives. For example, rather than direct benefits to the constituencies of MCs that are already predisposed to support the president, funds might be targeted to places represented by MCs whose support cannot be taken for granted. To the degree that our instrumental hypothesis concerns the interaction between executives and Congress, this view is roughly consistent with the principal argument in Arnold's *Congress and the Bureaucracy* (1979).

The third hypothesis stems from the literature on the cycling expected to take place during voting regarding who is and is not included in the majority coalition (e.g., Arrow 1951; Riker 1962; Mueller 1989; Tullock 1998). This theory predicts that any voting majority can be overturned by the minority shifting the policy alternative so as to split off a sufficient portion of the majority (Arrow 1951; Riker 1962; Plott 1967; McKelvey 1975; Mueller 1989). We argued in chapter 2 that the various theories of distributive politics

are all variants of how MCs are predicted to respond to the fundamental instability in democratic voting by creating some sort of
institution or decision rule (e.g., Shepsle 1979). These structures are
thought to account for much of the stability in decision making that
does occur by providing for more predictable membership in the
governing coalition. Baumgartner and Jones (1993: 13–14) argue
that the episodic changes they observe over long periods of time in
nuclear power, tobacco, urban, and other policies reflect the inher-
ent instability of collective decision making in Congress.[1]

Of course, because they are instrumental attempts to accomplish
policy objectives, such legislative institutions may themselves be
subject to cycling (Riker 1980). The same incentives described by
Arrow and others that lead MCs who are not part of the governing
coalition to try to split the current majority still hold. Parties, ideology, and committee systems may provide an impediment to thwart
efforts to split a current majority coalition. However, the incentive
to disrupt the governing coalition remains. The resulting implication is that one way for those who are not part of the governing coalition to become so would be to shift the relative importance of different institutional structures.[2] For example, given the context of the
cold war, one way for Republicans (the minority party in Congress
for virtually the entire period under study) to improve their status
was to shift the structure of decision making away from partisanship and toward ideology. Historical accounts of Congress describe
the ebb and flow of what is commonly called the Conservative
Coalition between Republicans and conservative (often southern)
Democrats that has periodically become manifest. The "cycling"
hypothesis would predict periodic shifts in the relative importance
of party versus ideology in structuring distributive politics in Congress. The timing of such shifts may be difficult to predict,[3] but one
would expect to see a pattern whereby an increase in the importance
of ideology in distributive politics is accompanied by a parallel
decrease in the importance of partisanship, and vice versa.

Because this analysis is exploratory, we do not specify any specific form of time dependence. Instead we adopt an approach that

allows for the relationships among variables to ebb and flow over time. We reestimate the statistical model twenty-eight times, each time including five years' worth of data. For each successive estimate, we drop the earliest year's data and add a year at the end. Thus our first estimates are based on 1963–67, then 1964–68, 1965–69, and so on. The result is a set of twenty-eight estimates for each parameter based on a five-year rolling average. We then plot these estimates over time with each estimate centered on the midpoint of the relevant five-year period. The resulting plots illustrate the changes that occur in the magnitudes of relationships among variables in our model over time. To facilitate comparison, we present standardized coefficient estimates here rather than the unstandardized estimates presented in previous chapters.

We should note that many of the estimates produced for each five-year period do not achieve traditional levels of statistical significance. This results in part from the real magnitude of some relationships but also from the smaller (five-year) sample sizes used to generate these estimates. Because of the difficulty in generating efficient estimates, we do not conduct statistical tests of the differences in coefficients we observe over time.[4] Our intent here is to describe the patterns that emerge from this analysis, focusing on general trends rather than specific coefficient estimates. While the confidence intervals around any one estimate might be fairly large, the chance is smaller that the overall patterns we observe arise strictly from random chance.

THE DYNAMICS OF BENEFIT DISTRIBUTION

We first examine the effect of previous defense committee representation on the subsequent distribution of military procurement awards. Figure 8.1 plots the estimated standardized coefficients relating House defense committee representation by a Democrat or a Republican to the subsequent distribution of military procurement awards. Again the estimates reported in this chapter are based on five years' worth of data, centered on each year. Thus an

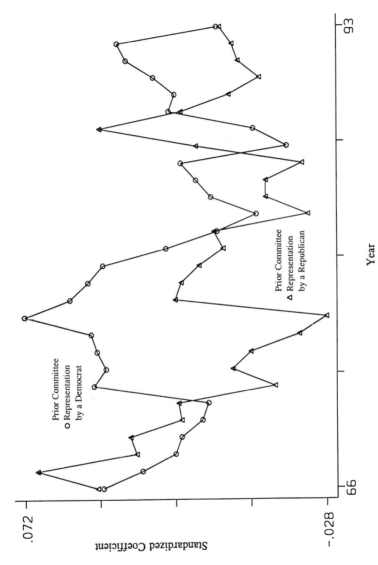

Fig. 8.1. Rolling average effects of prior House defense committee representation on change in per capita military procurement expenditures, 1966–1993.

estimate for 1975, for example, is based on estimating the entire multiequation model on data from 1973 to 1977.

Figure 8.1 shows that the relationship between previous representation on a House defense committee by a Democrat has a fairly consistent positive effect on the distribution of military procurement contracts over most of the period under study. The one exception is a decline in the magnitude of this relationship during the early and mid-1980s under the Republican president Ronald Reagan. States with Democratic representation on House defense committees did not receive larger military procurement benefits than states not so represented during Reagan's first term. We find little effect of House defense committee representation by a Republican during any period. Thus the general findings that states represented by Democratic, but not Republican, defense committee members receive additional defense procurement expenditures appears to hold fairly consistently over the entire period. That the ability of Democratic House defense committee members to obtain new military procurement dollars in their states weakens in the early 1980s may be due to the Republican presidency and Republican control of the Senate from 1981 to 1986. During this period, House defense committee Democrats still had the usual advantage of acting first on the appropriations for new and existing weapons systems. Therefore, they could challenge proposals that would advantage states represented by Republicans. Yet the Senate's ability to make changes in conference committee and the threat of a presidential veto may have been enough to block appropriations that disproportionately benefited the states of Democratic House committee members. The result appears to be that House defense committee members of both parties were unable to produce a statistically significant advantage in the distribution of military procurement expenditures during this period.

In the Senate we see a different pattern. Figure 8.2 shows that from 1966 to 1978 there is a clear positive relationship between changes in the distribution of per capita military procurement expenditures and a state being represented on a Senate defense

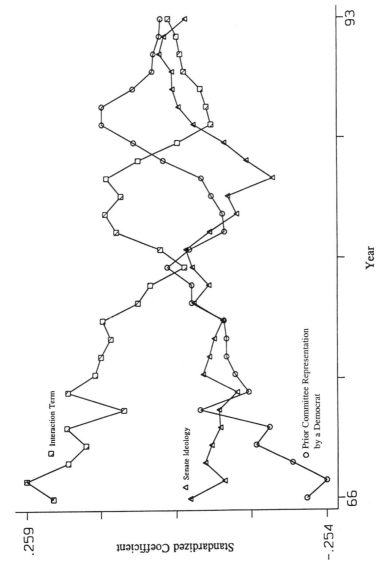

Fig. 8.2. Rolling average effects of prior Senate defense committee representation by a Democrat, Senate delegation ideology, and their interaction on per capita military procurement expenditures, 1966–1993.

committee by a Democrat *and* being represented in the Senate by a conservative delegation. In contrast, Democratic defense committee representation in the Senate for states sending liberal delegations to the chamber was associated with reductions in procurement benefits for this period. The same pattern reappears from 1980 to 1985. However, during the late 1980s, we see that representation on a Senate defense committee by any Democrat, liberal or conservative, appears to help a state receive additional military procurement dollars. What changes is the degree to which differences in the effect of Democratic Senate defense committee representation on the distribution of military procurement expenditures is conditioned on the ideological makeup of a state's Senate delegation. Figure 8.2 shows some periods in which conservative delegations with Democrats on a Senate defense committee do much better than their liberal counterparts. That gap between the two converges toward zero up to the election of Reagan and the GOP takeover of the Senate, at which point the pattern reappears. However, by the end of Reagan's second term, after the Republicans lost control of the Senate, we see some evidence that states with liberal Democrats on Senate defense committees outperformed their conservative counterparts.

We next turn to the direct effect of House delegation ideology on the distribution of military procurement benefits. First, recall that we found for the entire 1963–95 period that the ideology of a state's House delegation did not influence the distribution of military procurement awards. Figure 8.3 suggests that this may result more from the volatility of the influence of ideology on miliary procurement spending from than its absence. The House ideology effect is negative in the late 1960s, the mid-1970s, and again from 1988 to 1992. In between, the effect was either estimated at near zero or, from 1982 to 1985, as positive. This final finding supports what we have already seen: the distributive politics of military procurement spending deviated from the norm during the first six years of Reagan's administration.

Rather than try to explain every shift in the effect of ideology, we would like to draw attention to the finding that the ups and

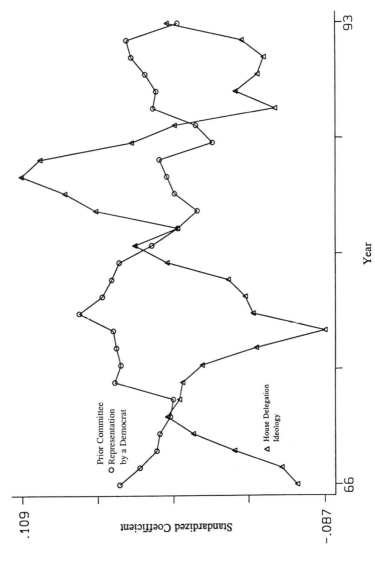

Fig. 8.3. Rolling average effects of prior House defense committee representation by a Democrat and House delegation ideology on change in per capita military procurement expenditures, 1966–1993.

downs associated with the influence of House ideology on the distribution of military procurement expenditures generally mirror fluctuations in the effect of Democratic defense committee representation. The effect of House Democratic defense committee representation fluctuates much less than does the effect of House ideology, but what movement there is appears to take place in conjunction with fluctuations in the impact of House ideology. This suggests that the conditional party on committee effect we find competes with House ideology to influence the distribution of benefits.

THE DYNAMICS OF HOUSE DEFENSE COMMITTEE REPRESENTATION

One of our key findings is that defense committee representation is related to states' economic interest in military procurement, as measured by the previous level of per capita military procurement expenditures. Figure 8.4 shows that over virtually the entire period, states with relatively higher levels of military procurement awards per capita were more likely to gain subsequent House defense committee representation. However, the figure reveals some fairly substantial swings in the magnitude of this relationship. The effect is small up to 1971, becomes much larger from 1972 to 1980, becomes negligible between 1980 and 1991, then returns to its large pre-1980 level after 1991. Previous levels of military procurement expenditures are admittedly a rough measure of constituency interest, but the analysis represented in figure 8.4 shows a volatile relationship between constituency interest in defense procurement spending in a state and obtaining defense committee representation in the House.

Turning next to the question of retention of House defense committee representation, our analysis finds little variation in the effects of prior representation by a Democrat or a Republican on a House Defense committee and current representation, even when conditioned by ideology. Figure 8.5 shows that states represented by either a Democrat or a Republican on a House defense committee are more likely to remain represented on a House defense

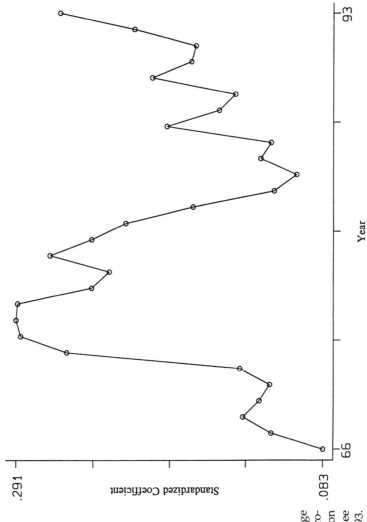

Fig. 8.4. Rolling average effect of prior military procurement expenditures on House defense committee representation, 1966–1993.

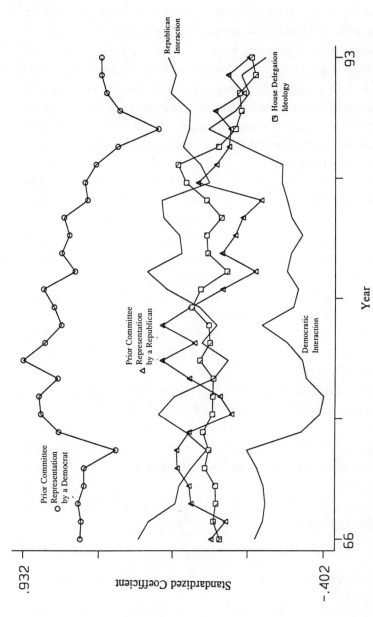

Fig. 8.5. Rolling average effects of prior House defense committee representation by a Democrat or Republican, House delegation ideology, and their interaction on House defense committee representation, 1966–1993.

committee compared to states that were not so represented. However, the effect is consistently stronger for Democrats. The effect for Republicans appears to be weakest after 1980, while the Democratic retention effect dips briefly in 1989.

Regarding the effect of ideology on House defense committee representation, figure 8.5 shows a consistent, though moderate, finding that states sending conservative delegations to the House are more likely to gain representation on a House defense committee. The only time this begins to break down is after the end of the cold war in the 1990s.

Interestingly, figure 8.5 shows that the effects of the interaction terms between prior defense committee representation by a Democrat or a Republican and House delegation ideology on subsequent defense committee representation in the House appear to mirror the direct effects of prior defense committee representation. Thus when the pure party effects of defense committee seat retention are strongest and positive in the House, the effects of these interaction terms provide a stronger negative counterbalance. For Democrats, the line for the direct effect of prior representation is always above that for the interaction term. This suggests that liberal Democrats are consistently more likely to retain their seats on defense committees, although the magnitude of the effects clearly shows that all Democrats are more likely to retain their seats than are any Republicans. The same pattern does not hold for the two Republican lines, suggesting that there are periods (mostly before 1980) during which more liberal Republicans are better able to retain defense committee representation and other periods (mostly after 1980) during which conservative Republicans do better at holding on to their defense committee seats.

THE DYNAMICS OF
SENATE DEFENSE COMMITTEE REPRESENTATION

In chapter 6 we reported that the impact of previous military procurement expenditures on Senate defense committee representation was positive and significant. Figure 8.6 shows, however, that the strength of this relationship at the beginning of the period under study was near zero. It steadily grew, however, to a high point in 1981. The strength of the relationship then declined during the first half of the Reagan administration but began to grow again after the Republican Party lost control of the Senate in the 1986 midterm election. The pattern represented in figure 8.6 roughly parallels the pattern for the House presented in figure 8.4.[5] In both chambers there appears to be an ebb and flow in the degree to which places that already have relatively high levels of military procurement spending increase their chances of being represented on congressional defense committees.

Looking next at the question of Senate defense committee retention, figure 8.7 shows a large and fairly stable impact of prior representation on a defense committee by a Democrat and subsequent defense committee representation. If there is any noticeable shift, it is a decline in the effect that begins after 1984 and bottoms out in 1987. By the early 1990s, however, the effect has returned to its previously high level.

The pattern for Republican Senate defense committee retention differs. First, the effect is always less than the effect for Democrats, a finding similar to that in the House. However, the gap between the effects of prior representation by a Democrat versus a Republican is smaller in the Senate than in the House, and from 1968 to 1971 and again from 1982 to 1987, the Republican and Democratic effects in the Senate are very close. It is unclear what might be responsible for this effect from 1968 to 1971, but the second period is again during the Reagan administration and for much of the period when Republicans controlled the Senate. Following 1987, the Republican retention effect moves downward, reaching its lowest levels in 1991 before recovering slightly in 1992–93.

Looking at ideology, figure 8.7 reveals no substantial direct effect of state Senate delegation ideology on the probability that a state would be represented on a Senate defense committee at the beginning of our time period. However, we see a steady increase

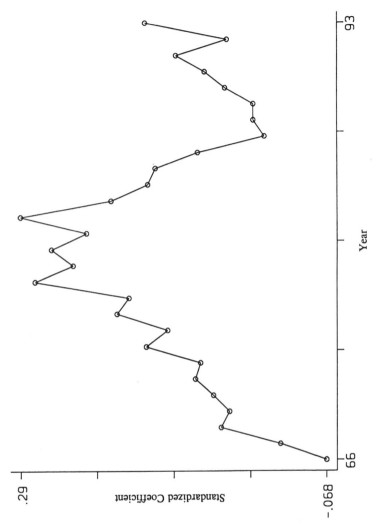

Fig. 8.6. Rolling average effect of prior military procurement expenditures on Senate defense committee representation, 1966–1993.

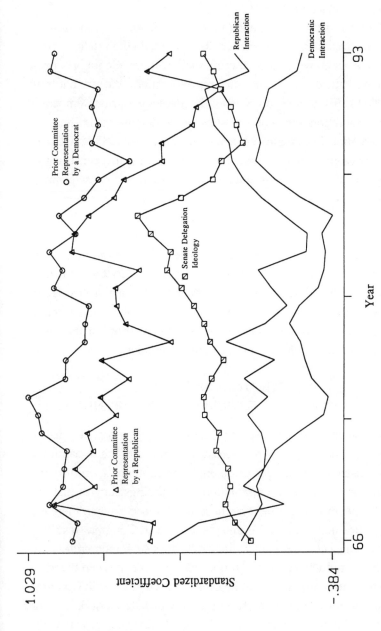

Fig. 8.7. Rolling average effect of prior Senate defense committee representation by a Democrat or Republican, Senate delegation ideology, and their interaction on Senate defense committee representation, 1966–1993.

in the effect of ideology up to 1984, after which it quickly declines to no effect again by 1987.

To see if there are trends in whether liberal or conservative Democratic senators were more likely to retain their defense committee seats, we created the interaction term (ideology × prior Democratic defense committee representation). We see that from 1966 to 1970 there is no effect of the ideology × prior Democratic representation interaction on subsequent defense committee representation. Starting in 1971 and continuing until 1985-86, we see a negative effect on this interaction term, meaning that conservative Democrats had more trouble holding onto their defense committee seats than did liberal Democrats. As the effect on the interaction term goes to zero, the direct Democratic representation effect also decreases. They move apart again in 1992–93. Looking at a similar interaction term for Republican Senate defense committee members, figure 8.7 shows that its effect was near zero for the entire time except during Reagan's first term, when this interaction effect is also negative. Like the House findings shown in figure 8.5, the effects of these interaction terms in the Senate mirror those of the direct effects of prior defense committee representation.

THE DYNAMICS OF THE DISTRIBUTIVE POLITICS OF DEFENSE SPENDING

We conclude by returning to the distributive moments, instrumental, and cycling hypotheses as they relate to the dynamics of the distributive politics of defense procurement spending and defense committee representation. Our findings suggest that distributive moments might be most likely to occur when there is a significant change in the presidency and in Congress resulting from an election. Krehbiel (1998) describes such moments as significant reductions in the gridlock gap that result when the ideological orientation of what he calls the pivotal voter in Congress shifts significantly away from the previous status quo.[6] For the period included in our study, Krehbiel's data suggest that the largest reduction in the gridlock gap occurred as a result of Reagan's first presidential victory.

Recall that Reagan won a rather decisive victory in 1980 over incumbent Democrat Jimmy Carter in the midst of an economic crisis and the Iranian hostage crisis. Reagan's late surge also helped to give the Republicans control of the Senate for the first time in many years and significantly reduced the Democratic majority in the House. Of any period included in our data, this clearly marks a time when a fundamental shift in distributive politics could have taken place.

Looking back at our rolling average analysis, we see an increase beginning in 1980 in the targeting of benefits to states represented by conservative Democrats on the Senate defense committees as well as to states that sent relatively more conservative delegations to the House. The increased importance of ideology in the House and more narrowly among committee Democrats in the Senate lasts for almost the entire first term of Reagan's administration. This is consistent with the notion that distributive politics in Congress was temporarily altered during Reagan's first term such that the beneficiaries were states represented by members of the Conservative Coalition in Congress that Reagan repeatedly mobilized.

In both the House and the Senate, we also see that defense committee representation was less responsive to previous levels of military procurement spending in the first few years of Reagan's presidency than it tended to be both before and after. We also observe during Reagan's presidency that states sending conservative delegations to the Senate become more likely to achieve representation on Senate defense committees, although this was not true of the House.

This evidence suggests that the Reagan distributive moment may have produced a disruption in the normal process of defense committee representation. Note that committee representation by Democrats continued to influence the receipt of additional benefits during this time, but the normal reciprocal relationship between committee representation and benefit levels was temporarily disrupted on the committee representation side. This means that for a short time representatives from states without previous high levels of defense procurement had the same opportunity to obtain such representation as did representatives from states with high levels of defense procurement spending. Once represented on a defense committee, these states began to receive relative increases in per capita military procurement expenditures. Thus when the reciprocal equilibrium was restored, reestablishing the link between previous benefit levels and current committee representation that existed before Reagan's first term, it included a somewhat different group of states.

There are several fundamental points here. First, even though these disruptions were temporary, the autoregressive and interrelated nature of distributive politics revealed in our analysis means that even short-term shifts in one aspect of the model will be felt over a number of subsequent years and throughout the entire model.

Second, once new members acquire representation on defense committees, for there to be a payoff, particularly in the long term, they must reestablish the preexisting reciprocal relationship between defense committee representation and the distribution of military procurement expenditures. Now that they have gained entry to the distributive politics of military procurement spending, new defense committee members have every incentive to attempt to reestablish the reciprocal link between committee representation and benefits.

Third, the autoregressiveness of the distribution of procurement awards achieved its highest levels during Reagan's first term. Our initial expectation was that the reverse might be expected to occur during a distributive moment, with a reduced autoregression parameter indicating a period of more substantial shift away from the status quo whereby states receive procurement awards. However, this period of high autoregression may also signal that military procurement dollars did not have to be diverted from states that already received sizable benefit levels in order to "buy" more support from MCs on other issues. In other words, the distributive moment characterizing Reagan's first term may have been one in which the new governing coalition was sufficiently large and cohesive so that increases in military procurement benefits did not have to be widely dispersed to ensure passage of Reagan's larger policy agenda.

Overall, we see some evidence in our rolling average analysis that supports the notion that Reagan's first victory marked the beginning of a distributive moment. His victory ushered in a new governing coalition that not only changed the ideological location of Krehbiel's pivotal voter in Congress but also temporarily shifted the relationships among distributive politics variables. That the distributive politics of defense procurement appears to have returned in many respects to its pre-Reagan pattern of relationships suggests that this distributive moment produced a temporary shift in the equilibrium that more typically characterizes the distributive politics of military procurement.

Now let us consider the instrumental hypothesis. The expectation here is that military procurement benefits would be distributed in such a way as to garner the support of MCs that are not already predisposed to support the policy agenda of the president. Our preliminary evidence is mixed. The strongest supportive evidence is our finding that during the early and middle years of the Vietnam war, states sending Democrats to the Senate but without a Democrat on a Senate defense committee received disproportionately large amounts of defense procurement spending. Further analysis reveals that Senate Democrats on the defense committees during this period were predominantly conservative southerners. Thus the Democratic senators receiving greater increases in their levels of military procurement awards during this period were mostly northern liberals. This may represent an effort, particularly under the Johnson administration, to gain the support for, or at least temper the opposition to, the war among liberal Democrats in the Senate. This may have been necessary, or perceived so, because of the ability of a sufficiently mobilized liberal minority in the Senate to block military procurement legislation (Lindsay, 1991).

There is a second piece of evidence reported above that might support the instrumental hypothesis. Recall that we found the highest autoregressive function in the distribution of benefits during Reagan's first term. We speculated at that point that this may have reflected the strength of the Conservative Coalition during that time. We suggested that benefits did not need to be widely distributed beyond states already receiving high benefit levels because additional support for Reagan's policy agenda did not need to be "purchased." In other words, the absence of instrumental pressures during this period may have allowed new procurement funds to be distributed to places already receiving high levels of defense procurement expenditures.

In contrast, the instrumental hypothesis generates at least two other predictions that are not supported. First, if a president needs to buy votes for a larger policy agenda, rational theory would predict that he (someday she) would go after those votes that can be most easily acquired. In ideological terms, this suggests that funds would be targeted to states sending relatively moderate delegations to Congress. Moderates constitute swing votes in Congress and should be the ones whose support is most susceptible to being purchased. This suggests a nonlinear relationship between delegation ideology and the targeting of benefits. To test for this possibility, we reestimated the model, including our original measures of state delegation ideology for each chamber as well as new variables that square each of our chamber ideology measures. This analysis, however, failed to uncover any evidence that military procurement benefits were systematically targeted to ideological moderates.

The second hypothesis builds on the same logic, assuming that the easiest votes to acquire would be among members of the president's party. Again, however, we found no evidence in our overall period analysis, nor did we uncover anything in our rolling average analysis, to suggest that procurement awards were systematically targeted to states represented in Congress by partisans of the president's party.

What we are left with is one historical example during the Vietnam war that produces evidence consistent with the instrumental distribution of military procurement awards and a second historical example during Reagan's first term that produces some evidence consistent with the idea that such instrumental use of military procurement awards may not have been necessary. The remaining period appears to be characterized by somewhat lower, if any, levels of such instrumental pressures on the distribution of defense funds.

Finally, regarding the cycling hypothesis, we offer two points. The first one has been sufficiently described above that it only needs to be highlighted here. Reagan's first victory appears to have ushered in a period in which ideology relative to partisanship played a more important role in structuring distributive politics. This is consistent with the idea that the preexisting party-based equilibrium could be and was successfully disrupted in a manner that allowed Republicans previously outside the governing coalition to begin to benefit from the distributive process by joining with conservative Democrats.

Second, we reported early in our discussion of the rolling average analysis that there appears to be a sort of zero-sum tradeoff between ideology, on the one hand, and party-on-committee, on the other, in terms of which has more influence on changes in the distribution of procurement awards, particularly in the House. When the influence of one increases, the other appears to simultaneously decrease. This pattern suggests a more general conclusion that either party or ideology provides the primary emphasis for structuring decision making in Congress and that which is relatively more important at any point in time is in flux. Note, however, that we do not often see such fluctuations occurring in the House during our 1963–95 period. Figures 8.1 and 8.3 show that three basic swings took place. Thus the kind of cycling that might be occurring here is much less frequent than those who focused on the original problem regarding individual voters might have suspected (e.g., Arrow 1951). Shepsle (1979), Poole and Rosenthal

(1997), Aldrich (1995), Cox and McCubbins (1993) and others appear to be correct that institutional structures like political parties provide some stability to the policy-making process. However, stability does not mean the absence of change or disruption, and our evidence suggests that such shifts regarding what structures policy making do take place from time to time, at least in the House.

Our exploration of the dynamics of the distributive politics of military procurement between 1963 and 1995 provides evidence of at least one period of instrumental targeting of benefits and another somewhat clear example of a distributive moment. We also see some evidence of cycling between the importance of ideology relative to party in structuring changes in the distributive politics of military procurement spending and defense committee representation. What we see in our rolling average analysis and is captured in the overall period findings presented earlier in this book is that the distributive politics of military procurement has a fairly complex and dynamic equilibrium but an equilibrium nonetheless. That equilibrium is a distributive politics based largely on the majority party using the committee system to structure policy making. We see historical instances during which this equilibrium is disrupted, but the general pattern in the rolling average analysis is that after such a disruption takes place, the effects return to the overall pattern of relationships described in our general findings in chapters 5 and 6. Even the disruption of the Reagan era can be viewed as support for a party-on-committee distributive theory. Reagan's victory and the Republican control of the Senate for six years represent a break in the Democratic Party's control of congressional policy making, though not a complete reversal of party control. One interpretation is that ideology became more prominent during this period only because of the absence of clear party control of Congress.

CHAPTER NINE

THE IMPACT OF MILITARY PROCUREMENT SPENDING

Often left unaddressed in the study of distributive politics is its effectiveness and its resulting impact on, in this case, states. Is it effective in achieving national defense objectives? Is it effective in improving local economic conditions or bringing home bacon that incumbent MCs can take credit for? In this chapter, we examine the extent to which military procurement expenditures are distributed so as to be nationally or congressionally effective and the role played by distributive politics in shaping these effects.

EFFECTIVENESS HYPOTHESES

Not all aspects of the national defense and economic effectiveness of military procurement spending can be studied in the context of our research design. Those aspects that can be are whether military procurement expenditures are targeted to states with greater capacity for doing defense work, whether they are targeted to wealthy or poor states or states with high or low unemployment rates, and whether the economic capacity and wealth of states increase as a result of their having received military procurement expenditures. Six effectiveness of military procurement spending hypotheses are examined:

1. States that have greater capacity for producing defense products are the targets of military procurement expenditures.
2. Poor states are targets of military procurement expenditures.
3. Rich states are targets of military procurement expenditures.
4. States with higher unemployment rates are targets of more military procurement expenditures.
5. States that receive more military procurement expenditures experience greater economic growth.
6. States that receive more military procurement expenditures experience increases in their capacity for doing defense contracting.

We already know the answers to the first four hypotheses. States with higher levels of defense production capacity and wealthier states tend to be targeted for defense spending. Poorer states and states with more unemployed workers are not. These findings suggest that military procurement spending is effective in promoting national security and may be either effective or ineffective vis-à-vis local and national economic development. In terms of local economic development, it is effective in helping already wealthy places to become wealthier. It is not effective in helping poor places become wealthier. In terms of national economic development, it is effective if providing money to already wealthy areas contributes more to national economic growth than does contributing it to less developed places. However, military procurement spending would be ineffective from a national economic development perspective if increasing the economic inequality among states detracts from national wealth. We reconsider these conclusions after reporting on our tests of Hypotheses 5 and 6.

METHODS

To test Hypotheses 5 and 6, we reestimate the statistical model presented in chapter 4 and used to produce the analysis reported in chapters 5 through 8, this time adding two additional equations.[1] The dependent variables for the new equations are the state's level of per capita income and the state's unemployment rate for that particular year, respectively. The independent variables in each equation are a lagged value of each respective dependent variable, the level of military procurement contracts received in the state in the previous year, and the familiar set of region and year dummy variables included in our defense procurement equation. Thus each equation models change in per capita income and unemployment, respectively, as a function of the previous year's level of per capita military procurement awards.

We recognize that the specification of these equations is limited and that other factors may also influence changes in state economic conditions. The state economic development literature points to a number of such factors that may be at work (e.g., Brace 1993; Carsey, Rundquist, and Fox 1997). In defense of our approach, we offer the following points. First, much of the variation in these excluded factors is captured by the regional and year dummy variables. Thus, while we will remain ignorant of each factor's unique effect, their total effect on changes in economic conditions in states is nonetheless largely controlled for in our statistical model. Second, the state economic development literature is quite mixed regarding the effect of state-specific policies on general measures of state economies such as per capita income or state unemployment. In fact, in work using a subset of our data, we found that none of the six measures of state economic development policy initiatives had the expected impact on either state per capita incomes or state unemployment (Carsey, Rundquist, and Fox 1997). Third, our approach accounts for 96 percent of the variance in per capita incomes and 89 percent of the variance in state unemployment rates (see table 9.1, below). In sum, we believe these simple models provide a reasonable test of the impact of defense procurement expenditures on state economies.

Before we present our analysis, we should report that we explored the possibility that the impact that defense procurement expenditures have on state economies might be conditioned by whether a state was represented by a Democrat or a Republican on a House or a Senate defense committee. This seems consistent with Levitt and Poterba's (1994) finding that states represented by more senior majority party delegations experience greater economic growth. However, we found that military procurement expenditures have the same effect on per capita incomes (and noneffect on unemployment rates) regardless of whether a state is represented on a defense committee and regardless of whether it is represented on a defense committee by a Republican or a Democrat. Similarly, there is also no evidence that the targeting of funds to relatively wealthier states (and no targeting to states with higher unemployment) is conditioned by committee representation.

RESULTS REGARDING THE IMPACT OF
MILITARY PROCUREMENT SPENDING

Table 9.1 reports our findings for the 1963–95 period. It shows that consistent with Hypothesis 5 above, the coefficient linking the previous year's level of military procurement awards per capita to the current year's state per capita income is .223 ($p < .01$). Because the analysis controls for the previous year's level of per capita income, this estimate captures the effect of the previous year's level of per capita military procurement spending on the change in state per capita income. The model shows that receiving an additional $1.00 per capita in military procurement awards results in an increase in state per capita income in the following year of $0.22. Thus, on average, as a result of increases in per capita military procurement expenditures, there is substantial growth in a state's income.

The relationship between military procurement spending and state economic growth is also consistent with the argument that MCs would want to obtain a seat on a defense committee to promote local economic development. Recall, for example, that a state represented on a House defense committee by a Democrat in year T receives an average increase of about $17.00 per capita in procurement awards in year T+1. That $17.00 boost in turn leads to an estimated increase in state per capita income of about $3.75 by year

TABLE 9.1.

*Impact of Military Procurement Contract Spending on Changes in
State Per Capita Income and State Unemployment Rates, 1963–1995*

	PER CAPITA INCOME	UNEMPLOYMENT
Per Capita income$_{t-1}$	.961	- - - -
State unemployment$_{t-1}$	- - - -	.855
Per capita military procurement spending$_{t-1}$	.223	-.000005

NOTE: $N = 1,600$. Robust standard errors computed as suggested by Beck and Katz (1995). Estimates produced are part of a full model of seemingly unrelated regression equations. Results from the other equations are reported in previous chapters. This equation also includes a set of dummy variables to control for region and year.

$*p < .1, **p < .05, ***p < .01$

T+2. This $3.75 represents an economic growth stimulus that a House Democrat on a defense committee can claim credit for as he or she campaigns for reelection.

The autoregressive parameter for per capita income is .96, meaning that this onetime effect on per capita income continues to affect state economic growth for a long time. On average, a full $0.96 out of every $1.00 carries over from one year to the next. Thus, for example, a onetime boost of about $3.75 measured over a ten-year period adds up to more than a $31.00 increase in per capita income for a state. If the state is continuously represented on a House defense committee by a Democrat for that same ten-year period, the total effect on a state's per capita income is more than $183.00.

Our second major finding in this chapter is that Hypothesis 6 is not supported by our analysis. The level of per capita military procurement expenditures received by a state is not associated with decreases in state unemployment levels. The coefficient is near zero for the 1963–95 period. Thus while military procurement awards are associated with income growth in a state, they do not create job opportunities of the sort that affect a state's overall employment rate.

What do our tests of Hypotheses 5 and 6 suggest about the national security and economic effectiveness of military procurement spending? First, they add nothing to the conclusion about national security effectiveness that we have drawn from our targeting analysis. Military procurement spending appears effective by this criterion given that we find some evidence of procurement expenditures being directed to places with the capacity to produce the goods and services needed for the national defense. Second, the impact analysis in this section supports the conclusion that military procurement policy may be both effective and ineffective in terms of local and national economic development. Clearly, our findings here and in chapter 5 of a reciprocal relationship between military procurement spending and state per capita incomes, such that rich states are targeted for military procurement spending and get richer as a result, supports Russett's (1970) conclusion that defense procurement spending contributes to income inequalities among the states. In a cross-national study, Alesina and Rodrik (1994) find that greater income inequality tends to create pressure for additional redistributive spending, which in turn leads to lower levels of economic growth. If this is true, then our findings that military procurement spending is effective in producing local economic development for relatively wealthy states also suggest that less national economic growth occurs because of the increased gap between wealthy and poor states.

DISTRIBUTIVE POLITICS AND ECONOMIC GROWTH

That military procurement spending has a positive impact on state incomes does not necessarily mean that the distributive politics of defense procurement accounts for this impact. In this section we examine the proportion of military procurement spending's effect on state income growth that can be traced to distributive politics in Congress. The hypothesis that guides this analysis is that distributive politics, in the form of states represented by House committee Democrats getting more, accounts for a significant amount of the increase in per capita income produced by military procurement awards.

Figure 9.1 shows some of the paths of influence we uncovered in our analysis in chapters 5 and 6. The arrows represent the causal direction of influence among variables. The coefficients next to the arrows are standardized coefficients produced by running the five-equation model used to generate the findings for this chapter.[2] Thus, for example, the path linking per capita military procurement contracts at time t-1 to per capita incomes at time t reports a standardized coefficient of .025. This means that a one standard deviation increase in per capita defense contracts is associated with a .025 standard deviation increase in state per capita incomes, controlling for other factors.

First, consider the effect on state per capita income of state representation on a defense committee in the House by a Democrat. Starting with the simplest path, we see that the standardized coefficient linking previous House defense committee representation by a Democrat to subsequent defense procurement expenditures is .031. To determine the indirect effect of House defense committee representation by a Democrat on state per capita incomes, we can simply multiply the relevant coefficients along the path from previous House defense committee representation by a Democrat to state per capita income. The result is .031 × .025 = .000775. In other words, when the probability that a state is represented on a House defense committee by a Democrat increases by one standard deviation, two years later that state's per capita income is predicted to increase by .000775 standard deviation, or about $1.96. This increase in per capita income results from the added boost in defense procurement contracts that states receive as a result of committee representation.

Another way to interpret the indirect effect of House defense committee representation by a Democrat on growth in per capita

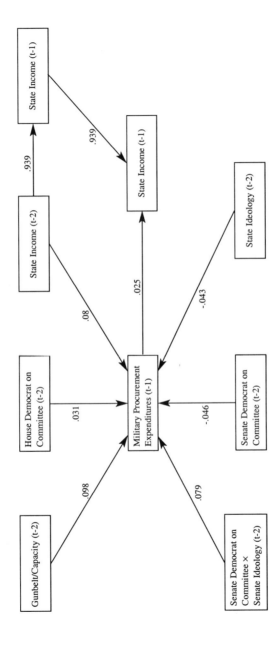

Note: *Path coefficients are standardized.*

Fig. 9.1. Path model of distributive politics effects on state per capita income with one-year and two-year lags, 1963–1995.

incomes is to consider what portion of the direct effect of procurement contracts on state incomes results from this indirect effect. This can be computed as a simple ratio of the indirect effect on state incomes that results from House defense committee representation by a Democrat compared to the direct effect of procurement expenditures on state income growth. Thus by dividing the indirect effect (.000775) by the direct effect (.025), we get the proportion of the direct effect of per capita procurement contracts at t-1 on state income growth at T that results from a state being represented on a House defense committee by a Democrat at t-2. That proportion is .000775 ÷ .025 = .031, or 3.1 percent. In other words, Democrats serving on a House defense committee can claim credit for, on average, 3.1 percent of the growth in state per capita incomes that occurs in response to military procurement spending.

So far we have only considered the most recent year's defense procurement contracts and only the previous year's House defense committee representation. However, we know that the distributive process is more dynamic than this. For example, recall that committee representation, the distribution of procurement expenditures, and state per capita income all exhibit autoregressive processes. As a result, any onetime effect of House defense committee representation by a Democrat, for example, will continue to be felt throughout the system for several subsequent years. Thus to fully grasp the effect of the distributive politics of military procurement spending on the relationship between procurement expenditures and subsequent growth in state per capita income, we must move farther back in time.

Figure 9.2 illustrates this by moving backward an additional step. The question remains the same: to what degree is the relationship between military procurement contracts and subsequent growth in state incomes the result of previous House defense committee representation by a Democrat. Working through the paths shown in figure 9.2, we conclude that, on average, 10.7 percent of the direct effect of procurement spending at t-1 on state per capita incomes at t results from the interactive effects of party and committee

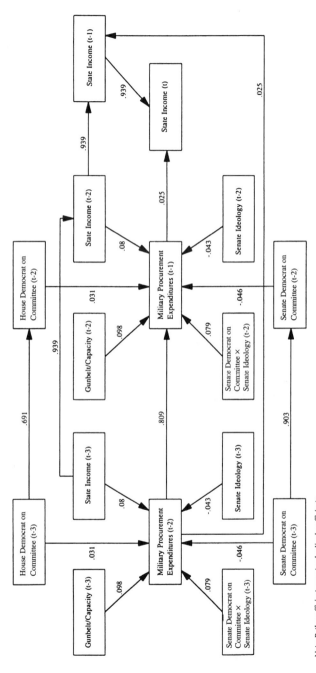

Note: Path coefficients are standardized coefficients.

Fig. 9.2. Path model of distributive politics effects on state per capita income with one-year, two-year, and three-year lags, 1963–1995.

representation that unfolds in the House at times t-3 and t-2.[3] To illustrate this conclusion using a hypothetical example, our model suggests that 10.7 percent of the growth in a state's per capita income that takes place in 1980 as a result of the level of defense procurement expenditures received by that state in 1979 can be attributed to whether the state was represented on a House defense committee by a Democrat in 1977 and 1978.

Making a similar argument for the indirect effect of the distributive politics in the Senate on state economic growth is more complicated because of the interactive relationship between Senate defense committee representation by a Democrat and Senate delegation ideology. As figures 9.1 and 9.2 remind us, we find direct effects of Senate defense committee representation by a Democrat and Senate delegation ideology on the distribution of per capita military procurement awards that are negative. However, the multiplicative interaction between these two variables has a positive effect on benefit distribution. Thus, in a path analysis like the one presented for the House, the two negative direct effects work to counter the positive interactive effect.

Looking again at figure 9.1, we can say that the indirect effect of Senate defense committee representation by itself on state incomes that results from its impact on military procurement expenditures is −.046 X .025 or −.00115. This means that a one standard deviation increase in the probability of a state being represented on a Senate defense committee by a Democrat at t-2 works through the distribution of military procurement expenditures at t-1 to actually lower state per capita incomes at t by −.00115 standard deviation, or about $2.91. Similarly, the effect of Senate delegation ideology at t-2 on state incomes at t is such that an increase of one standard deviation in Senate delegation ideology two years before results in a decrease in state per capita incomes of .001075 standard deviation, or about $2.72. However, the interaction between Senate defense committee representation by a Democrat and Senate delegation ideology has a positive effect that nearly counters these two negative effects. Figure 9.1 reports a standardized coefficient of .079.

Thus the indirect effect of a one standard deviation increase in this interaction at t-2, working through the distribution of military procurement expenditures at t-1, on state per capita incomes at t is .079 × .025 = .001975. This translates into an increase in state per capita incomes of about $5.00. Of course, talking about these three impacts in isolation is artificial because of the interactive effect that Senate defense committee representation by a Democrat and Senate delegation ideology have on military procurement benefits. One way to consider these effects is to imagine a one standard deviation increase taking place in all three. Under such an hypothetical, the net impact of Senate defense committee representation by a Democrat, Senate delegation ideology, and their interaction at t-2 would be to lower state per capita incomes at t by about $0.63.

It is similarly complicated to move back in time and to calculate the percentage of the effect of per capita military contracts on state incomes that results from the distributive effects in the Senate. However, looking at the overall net impact of the distributive effects in the Senate produces an effect of about −.0017, which in absolute value terms constitutes about 6.9 percent (1 − .0071 ÷ .0251) of the direct effect of per capita military contracts on state income.

Considering a third example, we next examine the growth in state incomes resulting from defense procurement spending that comes from defense procurement dollars being targeted to high-capacity states in the Gunbelt. Figure 9.2 shows that if we consider four time periods (t-3 through t), we find that 17.7 percent of the growth in state incomes associated with the receipt of defense procurement awards results from those awards being targeted to high-capacity states in the Gunbelt. This does not mean that state incomes necessarily grew at a higher rate in Gunbelt states or that procurement awards produce a higher rate of income growth in high-capacity states than in a non-Gunbelt state. Rather it means that, because procurement contracts go to high-capacity Gunbelt states and because such contracts cause income growth, the economies of these states benefit because the distributive politics of defense procurement targets benefits to states in the Gunbelt with the most capacity to produce military weapons.

To what degree does the distributive politics of military procurement spending cause rich states to get richer? This is a difficult question to answer. To begin with, figures 9.1 and 9.2 remind us that there is a reciprocal relationship between state per capita incomes and the distribution of military procurement expenditures. As a result, part (8 percent) of the growth in state incomes that results from receiving military procurement awards can be traced to the fact that those awards are more likely to go to states with higher per capita incomes to begin with. Obviously, as this unfolds over time, the model predicts that both the geographic distribution of procurement awards and the across-state variance in per capita incomes will become more polarized.

Similarly, we learned in chapter 6 that states with higher unemployment rates were significantly less likely to be represented on a House defense committee. Assuming that this applies equally to representation by either a Democrat or a Republican,[4] it would follow that because representation on a House defense committee by a Democrat pays off in terms of procurement awards and thus income growth, the party-on-committee-based benefit hypothesis that our study supports also contributes to a greater economic gap between states. Using the same sort of path logic described above, we can conclude that states with a one standard deviation higher rate of unemployment at times t-3 and t-2 can expect a level of per capita personal income in time t that is about $0.17 lower due to the party-on-committee distributive politics effect that characterizes defense procurement politics in the House.

THE DYNAMICS OF DEFENSE PROCUREMENT AND STATE ECONOMIC GROWTH

In this section we discuss a set of rolling average analyses similar to those presented in chapter 8. We focus on whether the nature of the relationship between the distribution of military procurement

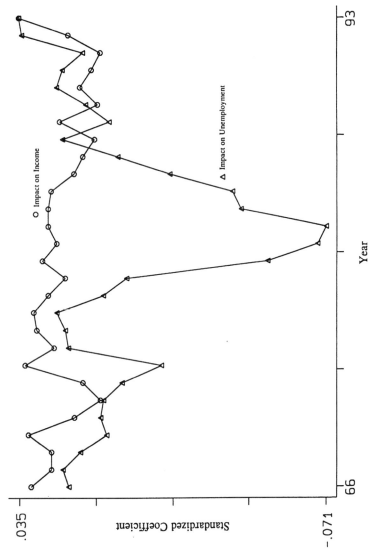

Fig. 9.3. Rolling average effect of prior military procurement expenditures on state per capita income and state unemployment, 1966–1993.

expenditures and state economic conditions changes over time. Figure 9.3 shows that the impact of defense procurement expenditures on per capita income has been fairly steady over the entire period, although it was somewhat smaller from the mid-1980s through the early 1990s.

The rolling average analysis regarding the impact of military procurement spending on state unemployment is much different. Figure 9.3 shows that for most of the period, additional per capita expenditures were not associated with changes in unemployment rates. However, in the midst of a recession early in Reagan's first term, higher levels of per capita military procurement spending are associated with subsequent reductions in state unemployment. Thus for this five-year period, military procurement spending resulted in lower state unemployment rates. This finding of a strong impact on unemployment under Reagan may represent evidence of the instrumental use of military procurement spending to generate support for Reagan's defense budget among working-class Democrats.

We have confirmed the findings of other studies that military procurement spending has a positive effect on state economic growth, although we have found no general effect of military procurement spending on state employment levels. We conclude that in terms of national economic development, military procurement spending can be judged both effective and ineffective. It is effective if greater national economic growth results from already rich areas getting richer. It is ineffective if the greater income inequality among states leads to decreased national economic growth. This latter argument, however, seems to have more support in the literature. From a national security perspective, our analysis suggests that the distribution of military procurement expenditures is effective.

We have also demonstrated that a significant part of the effect of military procurement spending on state economic growth can be traced to the distributive politics of military procurement spending. All states that received military procurement expenditures experienced income growth. But because representation on a House defense committee by a Democrat results in significantly larger increases in military procurement expenditures, states that are so represented experience significantly more income growth. It is this added growth in per capita incomes that Democratic MCs on House defense committees can claim credit for when facing reelection.

CHAPTER TEN

CONCLUSION

This book is about political scientists' theories and hypotheses about the nature of distributive policy making in Congress, focusing specifically on the persistent empirical anomaly of military procurement spending. The theories, we argue, are versions of distributive politics theory; the hypotheses are theoretical projections that should be valid if distributive politics theory is valid; and the anomaly is that these hypotheses have tended not to be supported in studies of military procurement spending.

We began by trying to show that earlier studies of the distributive politics of military procurement spending (including some of our own) were limited in conceptualization and design and that a new empirical investigation was justified. Our study suggests that there is a distributive politics of military procurement spending, although it takes a form more complicated than previously considered. In other words, we have resolved the anomaly relative to military procurement, therefore concluding that distributive theories of legislative policy making merit reinvigorated attention.

MAJOR FINDINGS

The geographic distribution of military procurement spending tends to favor states represented on House and Senate defense

committees by Democrats and on Senate defense committees by conservatives. None of the single-cause distributive theories, such as the
pure party-, ideology-, or committee-based theories, can by themselves account for the distribution of military procurement expenditures. Rather, aspects of these theories have to be combined to predict
the geographic distribution of military procurement expenditures. So
Shepsle and Weingast (1995), Rohde (1991), Krehbiel (1991), Hall
(1996), and others appear to be on the right track when they suggest
that a combination of these theoretical approaches is necessary to
explain congressional policy making.

However, our analysis suggests that standing committees in
Congress have played and continue to play an important role in
congressional policy making. There is a reciprocal relationship
between the distribution of military procurement expenditures and
defense committee representation. Areas represented on defense
committees tend to receive more military contracts, and MCs from
areas that get more defense contracts are more likely to obtain seats
on defense committees.

An additional element of the hybrid form of distributive politics
we have uncovered is that military procurement expenditures also
are targeted in part to geographic areas with greater capacity to per-
form military work. In this sense (and perhaps not others), distributive politics appears, from a national security perspective, an effective way of distributing military procurement expenditures.

States that receive more military procurement expenditures tend
to experience greater economic growth than other states. That some
portion of this growth results from distributive politics means that
the distributive politics of military procurement spending is also
effective in fostering local economic development.

An effect of the distributive politics of military procurement
spending is that rich states get richer. This tendency could be consistent with national economic growth if it could be shown that
investing in rich areas produces more national economic growth
than does investing in poor areas. But the same rich-get-richer tendency could also be inconsistent with national economic growth if

Russett (1970) is correct that greater inequality in the wealth of states, which military procurement spending results in, slows or reduces national economic growth. Thus whether the distributive politics of military procurement spending is effective from a national economic perspective depends on whether increased inequality has less of a negative effect on economic growth than investing in rich rather than poor parts of the United States has a positive effect.

Finally, it appears that for most of the 1963–95 period, the "normal" structure of distributive politics is one in which the majority party makes use of the committee system to foster the targeting of defense procurement expenditures to the advantage of majority party MCs on defense committees. This equilibrium appears to have been disrupted somewhat in the Senate during the early phases of the Vietnam war and more generally in Congress during the first term of the Reagan administration. In the 1960s the beneficiaries of this disruption were states represented by liberal Democrats in the Senate. In the 1980s the beneficiaries were states represented by conservatives of both parties. In both periods the effect of MC ideology on the distribution of military procurement expenditures increased at the expense of party. We conclude from this that party and ideology, while no doubt related, represent two competing forces that provide some structure to congressional decision making as MCs face the collective action problems presented by distributive politics.

Our findings are based on the analysis of a single policy area—defense procurement—during a specific period—1963–1995. This suggests that the tendency for places represented by Democrats on House defense committees and Democrats and conservatives on Senate defense committees to benefit from military procurement spending should be expected to continue only if Democrats have control of the House and the Senate. If they do not, our thinking suggests that Republican control of committees will result in a reversal of distributive beneficiaries so that areas represented by Republicans on House defense committees will increasingly benefit. In addition, if our findings can be generalized, our model should be expected to explain policy making in other policy areas for the same period. However, as we elaborate below, one big contingency may underlie this latter prediction: the policy benefits may have to be worth fighting for. If they are not, our results may not hold. Of course, it is also possible that our pattern of findings holds regardless of the level of benefits to be gained. We consider these possibilities next.

IMPLICATIONS

What do our findings mean? First, military procurement spending is less of an anomaly vis-à-vis distributive politics theory than political scientists have believed. Our findings are clearly inconsistent with the argument that "another kind of theory," such as some kind of public good or public regarding theory in which (say) military bureaucrats dominate elected politicians in making military procurement decisions, is needed to explain policy making in this area. To the extent that military bureaucrats make the decisions about the geographic location of military contracting, our findings suggest that they are responsive at least in part to majority party members on defense committees. Our analysis assures us that distributive politics is not the only factor affecting the geographic distribution of defense expenditures: we see clear evidence that local industrial resources and a history of previous defense contracting also have considerable influence. But distributive politics in the hybrid form that we have identified is clearly one of the influential factors, and this is enough to dismiss the so-called anomaly of military procurement spending. Thus our analysis suggests that the mixed findings of earlier studies of military procurement spending are the result of methodological shortcomings like those discussed in chapter 3 and not of the reality of defense contracting. One can pick particular years in which patterns like ours do not occur. Also, one can measure military procurement benefits as levels of expenditures rather than year-to-year changes or conduct a case study of a specific weapon system and, as a result, reach different conclusions. But we have established that over time and at several different levels of analysis (states, congressional districts, and counties),[1] our general pattern of results hold.

Second, we began our study by noting that there have been three major conceptualizations of distributive politics in the literature. Lowi's view relates policy processes to policy outcomes, mixing process and outcome criteria in identifying the domain of distributive policy making. He was, of course, thinking about omnibus pork barrel policies such as military procurement bills. Lowi's distinction between distributive politics and policy and regulatory and redistributive politics and policy rests on the amount of conflict involved in making each type of policy. Lowi argues that distributive politics as a process results from the nature of distributive policies. Because benefits from distributive policies could be subdivided almost infinitely, they would not be the subject of great partisan or ideological conflict. Rather, for their own electoral purposes, individual MCs can peel off pieces of the policy, "unit by small unit, each unit more or less in isolation from other units or any general rule." Distributive policies "are policies in which the indulged and the deprived, the loser and the recipient, need never come into direct confrontation" (Lowi 1964: 690). Thus distributive policies should be found to evidence little partisan or ideological conflict. In the more conflictual regulatory and redistributive contexts, ideological and partisan coalitions, often involving the president and other formally noncongressional actors, are more likely to be involved.

Wilson's (1973) interpretation of distributive policy making emphasizes the outcomes as the defining characteristic of distributive policy. His typology distinguishes four types of policies based on whether they have broad or narrow distributions of policy benefits and broad or narrow distributions of policy costs. Distributive policies are those with narrow distributions of benefits and broad distributions of costs. Thus Wilson clearly separates process from outcome in identifying the distributive domain.

The third approach, which served as the primary guide for our analysis, stresses the process of legislative targeting of policy benefits (Rundquist and Ferejohn 1975; Arnold 1979). This view of distributive politics hypothesizes that distributive processes leave evidence of their operation in the way that policy benefits are targeted and committee representation is determined. The original focus was on a committee-centered distributive theory, which, for example, postulates that if making policy that involves the distribution of money is committee centered, it will result in committee members' constituencies benefiting more than nonmembers' constituencies. The other distributive theories examined in this book, the party based, ideology based, and universalism based, have the same logic but posit different legislative processes. Thus this approach emphasizes process over outcome in defining distributive politics.[2]

In light of these varying ways of defining distributive politics, our resolution of the "anomaly" of defense procurement—a party-on-committee-cum-Senate ideology bias to the distribution of military procurement expenditures—may be interpreted as follows. First, à la the pure targeting view of Rundquist and Ferejohn, the anomaly disappears. There is a congressional bias that shows up in targeting; it is just different from what is predicted by the pure committee-centered hypothesis. For the mixed Lowi-like definitions, we find evidence of distributive targeting, but the evidence of party- and ideology-based targeting represents a challenge to Lowi's definition because, even though these are congressional processes that influence the distribution of expenditures, he argues that distributive policy making would not be conflictual enough to evidence partisan or ideological influences.

One interpretation of our findings is that the geographic distribution of military procurement expenditures reflects plenty of partisan and ideological conflict. The conflict is between geographic areas over military contracts and representation on defense committees. Our analysis suggests that the winners of this conflict tend to be members of the majority party, rich states, high-capacity states, and states that send more conservative MCs to Congress. Thus our analysis shows military procurement spending to be subject to the same kinds of conflicts that characterize other policy areas—for example, Lowi's redistributive and regulatory policies—and is typical of American politics generally. So either Lowi was wrong and not all divisible policies will be decided in nonconflictual distributive processes, or he was wrong about military procurement policy being a distributive policy. The kind of committee-, party-, and ideology-based distributive politics that we have found in military procurement spending may reflect the fact that this distributive policy is much more lucrative than other types of distributive policy (e.g., agricultural subsidies). Therefore, unlike other distributive policies, military procurement policy is worth competing for. And when something is worth competing for in mid- to late- twentieth-century American politics, that competition is generally structured through committees by parties or ideology that often produce benefits for the rich relative to the poor.

With regard to Wilson-like outcome-based definitions of distributive policies, our findings gain some additional meaning and the explanation of the military procurement anomaly gains a new insight. Again, the pattern we have discovered suggests that military procurement policy does not evidence the low levels of conflict that should be expected of the policies with narrowly distributed benefits and broadly distributed costs in Wilson's typology. Here we have widespread costs and narrowly targetable benefits but evidence of partisan and ideological competition. Why?

One possibility is that military procurement spending involves so much money that parties and ideological blocs find it beneficial to compete for chunks of it, particularly given that areas that end up being targeted for receiving military procurement expenditures experience faster economic growth than other areas. The tendency for military procurement spending to promote faster economic growth makes it worthwhile for partisan and ideological groups to compete for committee representation and for military procurement benefits to be targeted to their areas. Wilson is not mistaken for having scholars consider policy impacts, but those who use his framework may be misled if they assume that military procurement spending fits in the narrow benefits/broad cost cell because of the potential impact of military procurement spending on local economic development. In other words, regardless of whether a policy is an omnibus package of divisible and separately targetable programs, parties and ideological groups will compete over it if the policy's economic impact is great enough.

Envision a continuum from policies with low levels of impact on local economies to policies with high levels of impact on local economies. If one assumes that, ceteris paribus, most MCs want to contribute to the economic growth of their constituencies, it follows that (1) they would be more likely to pursue the enactment of policies with high local impact than of policies with low local impact and (2) because more MCs would be in pursuit of high local impact policies, there would be more conflict (partisan and ideological) over which constituencies should benefit from high local impact policies. By analyzing the relationship between targeting and effectiveness, our study has allowed us to observe that distributive politics may move from a politics of broad costs and narrow benefits to a politics of broad costs and broad benefits based on how much impact the policy can have on local economic conditions.

Of course, another explanation is that all or nearly all distributive policies reflect the partisan and ideological divides in Congress, not just those with large price tags or that have a significant impact on local economies. In this case, both Lowi's and Wilson's approaches would be wrong in assuming that party and ideology do not characterize policy making regarding distributive policies. Exploring this possibility, however, will have to wait for the next book!

By constructing a new study of the distributive politics of military procurement spending, we have been able to both dismiss an important anomaly in the distributive politics literature and to refine the understanding of distributive politics. We have provided evidence that distributive politics can account for policy making in a policy area that has a high level of potential impact on both the national security and local economic development. We have also shown that distributive politics is more effective vis-à-vis both the national security and local economic development than its detractors have contended.

APPENDIX A

The model outlined in chapter 4 is a set of simultaneous equations estimated on data pooled across geographic units—in this case, states—over time. Thus we are faced with all the problems of simultaneous equation models (see Bollen 1989) and pooled cross-sectional time series models (see Stimson 1985; Hsiao 1986; Beck and Katz 1995; Finkel 1995). We model all reciprocal relationships, or relationships where two variables are believed to cause each other, using lagged values of the variables under consideration. We do so because we believe that the distributive process takes time to unfold. For example, an MC gaining representation on a relevant committee will not be able to direct an instant increase in benefits back to his or her constituents. Rather any benefits that result should not show up until the following year.

Although we model the substantive relationships as reciprocal but taking place through lagged values and not as simultaneous, exogenous shocks or some unmodeled factors may still result in some contemporaneous correlation between the dependent variables. This correlation will manifest itself as contemporaneous correlation among the residuals of the equations as they have been defined in the model. To incorporate those correlations into the analysis, we estimate the equations simultaneously as a set of seemingly unrelated regression equations (see Bollen 1989). This improves the efficiency of the estimates. Pooled time-series data often evidence autocorrelation within the dependent variable. As noted in chapter 4, we treat this expected autoregressive nature of each dependent variable as something to be modeled rather than "fixed," and we do so by including lagged values of each dependent variable in its own equation. After controlling for the previous level of a dependent variable, the influence of each additional regressor can be interpreted as that regressor's effect on the change in the dependent variable from its previous value. Including lagged values of the dependent variables as regressors also allows us to estimate the cumulative effects of any regressor on each dependent variable.

The pooled nature of the data requires that we control for potential time and/or unit effects (Stimson 1985). We employ fixed effects models in which we include a set of eight dummy variables that represent regions of the country in every equation along with year dummy variables in the benefits and impact equations. The region dummy variables control for any systematic difference in levels of the dependent variables that exist across regions that are not captured by the other state-level independent variables. The year dummy variables capture any average year-to-year change that takes place nationwide in defense spending or need. This prevents the raw buildups and build-downs in defense spending from artificially contributing to the explanatory power of other independent variables in the benefits equation. It also controls for national cycles in income growth and unemployment in the need equations. We also estimate robust standard errors, following the method recommended by Beck and Katz (1995).

Our committee representation variables are dummy variables indicating whether the MC representing a particular geographic place is on a relevant committee. There is disagreement regarding how to respond when one or more of the equations in a set of simultaneous equations has a dichotomous dependent variable (see Bollen 1989; Browne and Arminger 1995). One could calculate a matrix of polychoric correlations and use this to estimate a structural model using a program such as LISREL or AMOS. In practice, however, this approach often results in a nonpositive definite matrix, which proved to be the case in our analysis. When this happens, the researcher is left unable to estimate the model.

An alternative is to ignore the dichotomous nature of these variables. Several studies suggest that if the dichotomous dependent variables are not overly skewed, the impact on the parameter estimates is minimal. Individual coefficient standard errors may be inflated, but this only results in making it more difficult to achieve statistically significant coefficient estimates. Because we estimate robust standard errors and because our two committee representation dummy variables are not dramatically skewed,[1] we opt for this second strategy.[2]

Appendix B

In chapter 4 we devote a fair amount of time to the question of whether the state is an appropriate unit of analysis for our study. As a check, we present in this appendix a replication of the state-level analysis reported in chapter 5 through 8 using data at the congressional district and county levels. This analysis is compatible with our state-level findings in most instances. Where the results vary across levels of analysis, they do so for readily understandable reasons. Thus we are confident in the state-level findings we reported.

Tables B.1 through B.3 report the results for our three-equation model. Each table first repeats the findings reported in chapters 5 and 6 regarding each dependent variable for the entire period under study. Because county- and district-level data are not available before 1983, the second column of each table repeats the state-level analysis for the 1983–95 period. The third and fourth columns present a similar analysis at the district and county level, respectively. There are a few differences worth noting at this point. First, the district-level and county-level analyses only include data up to 1994. Second, we did not have a county- or district-level measure of unemployment. Third, the county- and district-level analyses include state dummy variables rather than regional dummy variables in order to capture the pooled nature of the data. Fourth, our measure of capacity at the state level is GSP due to manufacturing. Such a measure does not exist at the county or district level. As a replacement, we measure capacity as per capita earnings from electronics and high-tech manufacturing.

Table B.1 reports the results of the influence of factors on the geographic distribution of military procurement expenditures. The first thing to note in table B.1 is the differences in the state-level findings for the two periods. Given our previous results (Carsey and Rundquist 1999a) and what we report in Chapter 8, this is not surprising. The distributive politics of military procurement has undergone some significant structural shifts since 1963. First, our analysis here and previously (Carsey and Rundquist 1999b) finds an important shift in the early 1970s regarding the role played by Senate Democrats. Second, our analysis in this book shows that the distributive politics of defense procurement spending differed significantly during the Reagan administration compared to both the 1970s and the 1990s. Thus the differences between column 1 and column 2 in Table B.1 result from the different periods each one covers. Further, many of the effects in column 2 do not achieve traditional levels of statistical significance because the sample size is roughly one-third of that for the analysis in column 1. Also, the period from 1983 to 1995 ends up pooling data from the Reagan administration and the post-Reagan era, two periods in which the factors that influence the distribution of defense procurement expenditures differ. The result is that most of the effects that show up in subsequent analysis of the Reagan and post-Reagan eras cancel each other out in column 2 of table B.1.

Column 3 presents the results of the expenditure equation at the district level. Here the pattern of findings is quite consistent with what we find for the post-1972 period. We see that previous representation on a House defense committee by a Democrat has more than twice the effect on the subsequent distribution of military procurement expenditures than does such representation in the House by a Republican. The effect does not quite achieve statistical significance, but recall that the period being covered is relatively short

TABLE B.1.

Factors That Influence the Targeting of Per Capita Military Procurement Spending across States, Congressional Districts, and Counties

VARIABLE	STATE LEVEL, 1963–95 (CHAPTER 5)	STATE-LEVEL 1983–95	DISTRICT LEVEL, 1983–94	COUNTY LEVEL, 1983–96
Per capita military procurement contracts$_{t-1}$	.811(.031)***	.87(.02)***	.85(.04)***	.93(.02)***
House Democrat on defense committee$_{t-1}$	17.266(5.677)***	5.7(6.5)	23.0(14.4)	51.9(26.5)*
House Republican on a defense committee$_{t-1}$	6.067(7.117)	-4.2(10.8)	10.2(12.5)	51.3(27.8)*
Senate Democrat on a defense committee$_{t-1}$	-27.290(14.591)*	17.6(10.9)	15.4(22.7)	121.8(43.6)***
Senate Republican on a defense committee$_{t-1}$	14.032(7.927)*	18.3(12.0)	13.1(10.7)	-30.2(45.0)
Percentage of Democrats in House delegation$_t$	-.088(.136)	.10(.24)	-19.5(8.5)**	-35.5(16.2)**
Percentage of Democrats in Senate delegation$_t$	-.039(.099)	-.10(.28)	8.1(10.7)	38.9(39.1)
House delegation ideology$_{t-1}$	-.228(.238)	.08(.3)	-.55(.19)***	-1.7(.48)***
Senate delegation ideology$_{t-1}$	-.469(.176)***	-.20(.28)	-.25(.34)	2.1(.96)**
Senate Democrat on a defense committee x Senate delegation ideology$_{t-1}$	.813(.270)**	.19(.27)	-.32(.36)	-2.0(.80)**
Per capita GSP due to manufacturing$_{t-1}$	-.003(.004)	-.007(.005)	9.18(14.2)	-.976(18.3)
Gunbelt state	-4.027(20.959)	22.3(27.8)	- - - -	- - - -
Per capita GSP x Gunbelt state$_{t-1}$	.021(.009)**	.007(.013)	18.3(21.6)	29.9(24.8)
Per capita income$_{t-1}$	.009(.003)***	.005(.003)	.0003 (.00009)***	.04(.006)***
Percentage unemployed$_{t-1}$	1.171(1.755)	-1.9(2.1)	- - - -	- - - -
R-squared	.86	.88	.84	.53

Unstandardized coefficient (Standard Error).

*$p < .1$, **$p < .05$, ***$p < .01$

and includes a portion of the Reagan administration during which the distributive politics of defense procurement differed from the rest of the post-Vietnam era (see chap. 8 for a fuller discussion). We also find at the district level no evidence of a pure party or pure ideological effect on the distribution of defense procurement expenditures. We do uncover less support for the notion that expenditures will be targeted to places with greater industrial capacity, although this may be the result of having a different measure of capacity at the district level. One thing that consistently shows up in table B.1 is that places with relatively higher per capita incomes in the previous year receive significantly more military procurement expenditures per capita in the following year.

Column 4 of table B.1 reports the results at the county level. Again, the county-level analysis replicates fairly well our post-1972 state-level and district-level analyses. One discrepancy of importance is the finding that previous representation on a House defense committee by either a Democrat or a Republican has a positive and significant effect on the distribution of military procurement expenditures, with the estimate for previous Republican representation being larger. An important conclusion of Carsey and Rundquist (1999a) and of this book is that partisanship and committee representation interact to produce distributive effects. This finding at the county level for the House runs counter to that conclusion (though the findings for the Senate do not). Current work on the within-district electoral implications of distributive politics may hold the answer to understanding this discrepancy (Schmit 2000), but that is as yet unknown.

Table B.2 reports the results for the state-, district-, and county-level analysis of the factors that influence representation on a House defense committee. Here the findings at all three levels are quite consistent. One conclusion possible from examining the various columns in this table is that the direct effect of previous committee representation by a Republican is larger in the district- and county-level analyses compared to the state-level analysis and that this effect is less conditioned by ideology in the district- and

TABLE B.2.
Factors That Influence the Probability That a State, Congressional District, or County Is Represented on a House Defense Committee

Variable	State Level, 1963–95 (Chap. 6)	State Level, 1983–95	District Level 1983–94	County Level 1983–96
Per capita military procurement contracts$_{t-1}$	.00018(.00003)***	.0018(.00009)**	.00005 (.000003)*	.000001 (.0000004)***
Democrat on defense committee$_{t-1}$	.687(.052)***	.64(.15)***	.92(.02)***	.91(.014)***
Republican on defense committee$_{t-1}$	.138(.069)**	-.05(.20)	.73(.12)***	.78(.05)***
Percentage of Democrats in chamber delegation$_{t-1}$	.0002(.0002)	.0002(.0005)	.009(.008)	.011(.003)***
Chamber delegation ideology$_{t-1}$	.0017(.0005)***	-.0004(.0012)	.00018 (.0001)	.0003 (.00005)***
Democrat on defense committee x chamber delegation ideology$_{t-1}$	-.0022(.0008)***	-.003(.002)	.0003(.0003)	-.00026(.0002)
Republican on defense committee x chamber delegation ideology$_{t-1}$	.0035(.0011)***	.005(.003)*	.002(.0014)	.0012(.0005)**
Per capita GSP due to manufacturing$_{t-1}$	.00003(.000008)***	.00004(.00003)	.00025(.02)	-.00058(.0003)*
Gunbelt state	.143(.038)***	.19(.13)	-----	-----
Per capita GSP x Gunbelt state$_{t-1}$	-.000073(.00002)***	-.0001(.00004)**	-.003(.02)	.00007(.0003)
Per capita income$_{t-1}$	-.000001(.000004)	.000005(.00001)	-.00000001 (.00000006)	-.000001 (.0000003)***
Percentage unemployed$_{t-1}$	-.005(.0025)**	-.01(.006)	-----	-----
Size of House delegation (logged)	.051(.011)***	.107(.013)**	-----	-----
R-squared	.72	.73	.84	.80
Percent of cases correctly predicted	94			

Unstandardized coefficient (Standard Error).
*p < .1, **p < .05, ***p < .01

county-level analyses than it is in the state-level analysis. Under-standing the role of partisanship in House defense committee rep-resentation is important, and these somewhat different findings at different levels of analysis might provide some insight. However, the fundamental conclusion that places represented by MCs from the majority party have a higher probability of gaining and retain-ing such committee representation is sustained across all levels of analysis.

Table B.3 presents results for Senate defense committee repre-sentation. Much the same can be said about table B.3 that was said about table B.2, with two exceptions. First, the substate analysis fails to uncover a significant relationship between previous levels of per capital military procurement expenditures received by a place and the probability of that place gaining representation on a Senate defense committee. Second, the county-level analysis produces a negative effect of Senate delegation ideology on Senate defense committee representation—an effect that is positive at other levels of analysis. However, the most important point to address regard-ing table B.3 is whether it is appropriate to analyze Senate defense committee representation at the district or county level in the first place. For the county and district analyses, every county and dis-trict in a state receives the same value for the dependent variable—whether it has a senator on a defense committee or not. By defini-tion this variable can only vary across states or over time. However, all of the independent variables also vary within states for the dis-trict- and county-level analysis. Thus the independent variables include a large amount of variance that by definition cannot explain variation in the dependent variable. It is not uncommon in politi-cal science to have independent and dependent variables measured at different levels, but when this occurs, it is generally the depend-ent variable that is measured at the lowest level of aggregation. For our Senate representation analysis using district- and county-level data, that situation is exactly reversed.

From a more substantive perspective, it is not clear that Senate defense committee representation should be expected to respond

TABLE B.3.

Factors That Influence the Probability That a State, Congressional District, or County Is Represented on a Senate Defense Committee

VARIABLE	STATE LEVEL, 1963-95 (CHAP. 6)	STATE LEVEL, 1983-95	DISTRICT LEVEL 1983-94	COUNTY LEVEL 1983-96
Per capita military procurement contracts$_{t-1}$	.000074(.000036)**	.00012(.00007) p=.103	.0000005(.000005)	.0000003 (.0000006)
Democrat on defense committee$_{t-1}$	.934(.040)***	.897(.09)***	.73(.03)***	.82(.01)***
Republican on defense committee$_{t-1}$	.685(.055)***	.499(.15)***	.80(.03)***	.75(.02)***
Percentage of Democrats in chamber delegation$_{t-1}$	.001(.0002)***	.0006(.0005)	-.003(.020)	-.069 (.006)***
Chamber delegation ideology$_{t-1}$	.0035(.0005)***	.003(.0015)*	.004(.0007)***	-.001 (.0002)***
Democrat on defense committee x chamber delegation ideology$_{t-1}$	-.0043(.00065)***	-.004(.0018)**	-.003(.0006)***	-.004 (.0002)***
Republican on defense committee x chamber delegation ideology$_{t-1}$	-.0009(.0008)	.0008(.002)	-.002(.0005)***	-.002 (.0002)***
Per capita GSP due to manufacturing$_{t-1}$	-.000028(.000012)**	-.00003(.00002)*	-.004(.012)	-.001(.001)
Gunbelt state	-.0099(.047)	-.09(.12)	---	---
Per capita GSP x Gunbelt state$_{t-1}$	.000007(.00002)	.00004(.00005)	.009(.013)	-.0005(.001)
Per capita income$_{t-1}$	.0000057(.0000033)*	-.000004(.000008)	.00000009 (.00000007)	.0000025 (.0000004)***
Percentage unemployed$_{t-1}$	-.0007(.003)	-.0035(.0059)	---	---
R-squared	.67	.64	.73	.76
Percent of cases correctly predicted	91			

Unstandardized coefficient (Standard Error).

$*p < .1, **p < .05, ***p < .01$

to substate characteristics. One could argue that it might respond to a senator's reelection coalition rather than to the entire state (e.g., Fenno 1978; Schmit 2000), but our data set does not include any information that we could use to identify a senator's reelection coalition or test such a proposition. So, while we present table B.3 to be consistent with what is presented in this appendix and we suppose that the fact that most of the basic findings hold up at the county and district levels, we are quite skeptical of the utility of this particular analysis and interpret the findings shown with much caution.

In sum, we believe our findings presented at the state level present a reasonable picture of the distributive politics of military procurement spending. We argue in chapter 4 for the advantages of conducting this analysis at the state level. Here we have shown that there is little empirical evidence to suggest that we would reach fundamentally different conclusions about the nature of the distributive politics of military procurement spending than we present in this book were we to conduct the analysis at the county or district level. There remain important within-constituency distributive hypotheses that would require analysis at the substate (subconstituency) level, but they are beyond the scope of this study.

NOTES

CHAPTER 1

1. Although the findings reported in the text concern the distribution of military procurement expenditures among states, we have replicated the same analysis at the congressional district and county levels for the somewhat shorter period of 1983 to 1996 for counties and 1993 for congressional districts. This analysis is summarized in Appendix B. The pros and cons of using states, congressional districts, and counties as units of analysis in this study are discussed in chapter 4.

2. See Sandler and Hartley (1995: chap. 8) for a review of the arguments regarding the possible negative economic impacts associated with defense spending. See also Russett (1970).

3. They also report that some models of defense spending consider the relative costs of defense versus nondefense goods, though this factor is often dropped if inflation rates are assumed to be equal in both the defense and nondefense sectors of the economy.

4. The ranges for each of the four quartiles are calculated using all 1,650 observations in the data set (50 states × 33 years). This means that for any one year, the fifty states may not be equally divided into four categories. Determining the quartile ranges in this manner rather than separately for each year facilitates making comparisons over time while still illustrating differences among states.

5. These coefficients capture the degree to which the relative rank among states and distances between states, measured in per capita procurement awards, remain stable across periods of ten, twenty, and thirty years. Values close to one represent a strong correlation and thus a fairly

high degree of stability in the distribution of procurement awards, while values close to zero represent a weak correlation and thus less stability.

6. Left out of our study is any consideration as to whether the specific goods and services that are procured are in fact effective at providing for the national defense and whether those goods and services are produced at least cost. We also do not consider the issue of local national security effectiveness. Local effectiveness of national defense implies that some locations may, possibly should, benefit more from national defense than others. For example, Wall Street and Silicon Valley may have more to lose from a foreign invasion than does (say) Nebraska, and thus those places might be, possibly should be, better protected. However, this problem does not imply anything about the geographic distribution of military procurement expenditures but would be concerned more with the geographic distribution of troops and weapons along with the configuration of military forces and defense plans.

7. The implication is that such policy benefits reward previous electoral support or translate into votes in subsequent elections. Empirical tests of these hypotheses have been mixed, but recent work suggests evidence for both (Schmit 2000). We do not consider the electoral connection directly in this study.

CHAPTER 2

1. Some theorists lean less heavily on reelection seeking, assuming only that MCs may have a variety of legislative goals and policy preferences that may result from other reasons, many of which are unique or shared by only a few members (Shepsle and Weingast 1995).

2. Peterson's (1995) legislative theory of federalism, which he contrasts with the functional theory, is also a distributive theory.

3. A more complete treatment of the cycles, and thus instability, in outcomes of collective decision making predicted to result from a variety of voting procedures may be found in Mueller (1989).

4. Aldrich (1995: 30) defines policies as distributive if they "concentrate benefits in one district or a few but distribut[e] costs broadly, perhaps equally, across all districts." While consistent with how much of the distributive literature has treated the term since Lowi (1964), this differs from our definition of distributive politics as a process rather than as a descriptor of the geographic distribution of costs and benefits. However, this difference does not diminish the importance of Aldrich's general conclusion that parties are created in part to solve collective action problems associated with policy making involving the geographic distribution of policy benefits.

5. A wealth of literature dating back at least to *The American Voter* (Campbell et al. 1960) stresses the importance of party labels in mass voting behavior.

6. Ironically, an even purer ideological version of distributive politics would imply that benefits would *not* be distributed to constituencies represented by hawks because the motivation for supporting defense spending is ideological and not material. This would be consistent with finding no correlation at all between ideology and the distribution of military procurement expenditures.

7. Typically, the discussion of minimum winning coalitions in democratic decision making focus on the median voter (e.g., Mueller 1989). Kriehbel (1998), however, argues persuasively for a more general focus on what he calls the pivotal voter, which is the last voter needed to adopt a policy. Kriehbel argues that in the U.S. Congress, the structure of decision making generally requires more than a simple majority to pass a policy, with a level of support more typically at about two-thirds. Thus Kriehbel's pivotal voter is not usually the median voter but rather the last voter needed to form a large enough bloc to pass the policy. However, the point that legislators that could be part of a stable minimum winning coalition could benefit from doing so is unaffected by Kriehbel's analysis.

8. This definition is similar to what Weingast (1979) refers to as "reciprocity."

9. Constituency economic interest has also been defined as restricted to the economic interests of the active electorate in an MC's district (Weingast and Marshall 1988) or simply in terms of MC committee requests (Weingast 1979), although such definitions also lack explication regarding the nature of the economic interest that motivates the active electorate or structures committee assignment preferences.

CHAPTER 3

1. Stein and Bickers (1994) examine change in the distribution of non-defense expenditures by identifying new programmatic expenditures each year. However, their approach precludes analysis of cumulative effects.

CHAPTER 4

1. We also consider alternative specifications of the same basic model across the two chambers in subsequent chapters and report any differences we find.

2. This skepticism proved well founded in our case as we uncovered no evidence that military procurement expenditures significantly influenced this broad measure of state industrial capacity.

3. The basic structure of the model parallels what Finkel (1995) calls a cross-lagged model. Each equation includes some additional control variables and a set of dummy variables that control for the pooled time-series nature of the data. The rationale for these dummy variables, along with a discussion of a number of other methodological issues, is presented in Appendix A.

4. For an overview of the analysis of interactive effects, see Jaccard, Turrisi, and Wan (1990).

5. Note that we lose the first year's worth of data in our analysis because each equation includes lagged values of several variables in the analysis. Thus our working sample size for most of the analysis is 1,600.

6. See the previous section for a discussion of the implications of subcontracting for this study.

7. For example, in 1999 thirteen states sent two Democrats to the Senate and eighteen states sent two Republicans.

8. Statistical estimates that accounted for the Republican control of the Senate in the early 1980s or the Republican takeover after the 1994 elections did not produce substantively different results.

CHAPTER 5

1. One could go even further to argue that if there is no difference between chambers, all four coefficients should be equal to each other. Most distributive theories are silent on the potential differences between chambers. Thus we leave it as an empirical question.

2. Again, we measure this as the proportion belonging to the Democratic Party because it was the majority party in Congress for the bulk of the thirty-three years under study.

CHAPTER 6

1. One might consider conducting a similar analysis predicting the partisan composition and ideological composition of each state's House and Senate delegation. Party- and ideology-based distributive theories posit that because places represented by majority party or conservative members tend to be targeted for benefits, states that benefit will seek representation by majority party members and conservatives. We have explored such models, and our analysis reveals no evidence of a recipro-

cal relationship between military procurement expenditures and either state delegation partisanship or ideology.

2. The relevant test is an F-test of equality between the parameters on the two variables in question in each equation. For the House, the resulting F statistic is 48.01 (df = 1,1567; p < .01). For the Senate, the F statistic is 22.93 (df = 1,1567; p < .01).

3. We have already discussed the problems involved in distinguishing MC ideology from partisanship.

4. One could still argue that MC ideology is just an intervening variable between constituency ideology, separate from constituency interest, and defense committee representation. However, we believe that our effort here makes some progress toward separating constituency economic interest from MC ideology.

CHAPTER 7

1. Of course, a number of other variables influence the distribution of military procurement contracts. We have estimated a fairly complex statistical model that includes measures for several factors and controls for region and for year. Thus while examining the cumulative effect predictions from our model is important for understanding the nature of distributive politics, a simple prediction like this considers only the effect of previous committee representation and the autoregressive nature of benefit distribution. It does not consider (i.e., it holds constant) all of the other factors in the statistical model that also influence changes in per capita procurement award levels in states from year to year. Thus these estimates are meant as heuristic devices and may not literally apply. For example, the estimates generated when a state has a conservative Senate delegation but is not represented by a Democrat on a Senate defense committee are obviously exaggerated. For another example, while Colorado experienced a level of growth in per capita military procurement expenditures like that described here during the 1980s, its level of procurement awards actually declined sharply in the 1990s even as it retained House defense committee representation by a Democrat. Other factors included in the analysis caused this decline, although our estimates would still suggest that had Colorado lost its committee representation, the decline in actual per capita procurement spending would have been even larger.

2. Purists in the time-series tradition will fault us for including the 1995 data in the analysis used to produce the subsequent forecasts for 1995. We understand and generally sympathize with the conceptual point being raised here. However, we found that after rerunning the analysis

excluding the 1995 data and then comparing actual and predicted values for 1995, no substantive changes in our conclusions resulted.

3. The actual value of military procurement contracts reported for Virginia in 1995 was more than $2,000 per capita. This is substantially higher than the overall mean for this variable for the other forty-nine states in 1995 ($224) and for all states for the entire period excluding Virginia in 1995 ($336).

CHAPTER 8

1. Poole and Rosenthal (1997) find that a simple ideological structure underlies congressional roll call voting. They assert that this constitutes empirical evidence that the instability predicted by spatial models of voting does not take place to the degree those theories anticipate. Of course, one might counter that much of the ideological structure they uncover falls along party lines, which might suggest that parties, rather than ideology, are responsible for the stability they find.

2. This view is not unlike Riker's (1980) view of partisan realignment or his and others' views of the nature of electoral conflict as causing heresthetic change in the issue space of an electorate (Riker 1990; Carsey 2000).

3. Certainly one would look to significant shifts that might result from an election. However, numerous other precipitating events may also spark such shifts.

4. Also, conducting a large number of statistical tests in this exploratory analysis would be somewhat disingenuous, because to do so would amount to a search for differences with a post hoc application of statistical tests to those that are uncovered.

5. The only difference is that the swings in the magnitude of the relationship appear to be sharper and happen slightly sooner in the House compared to the Senate. We suspect that this reflects the longer term of office in the Senate.

6. Briefly, Krehbiel's theory is similar to the median voter model except that Krehbiel argues (as do others) that passing legislation in Congress necessarily requires more than a simple majority or minimum winning coalition. For legislation to make it through the committee system, through both chambers, and past the president generally requires a voting coalition in Congress of approximately 65 percent of the members. The pivotal voter is that voter who allows a majority to reach that 65 percent level. Thus the pivotal voter in Krehbiel's theory plays much the same role as does the median voter in traditional spatial models by making the difference between adopting the new proposal or retaining the status quo.

CHAPTER 9

1. Note that none of the substantive findings reported in chapter 5 or 6 change when these two equations are added to the statistical model.

2. The parameters are presented in standardized form to facilitate comparison and to simplify the calculation of the indirect effects of committee, party, and ideology on changes in state per capita income.

3. The relevant paths are House Dem on Committee (t-2) to Military Procurement Expenditures (t-1) to State Income (t); House Dem on Committee (t-3) to House Dem on Committee (t-2) to Military Procurement Expenditures (t-1) to State Income (t); House Dem on Committee (t-3) to Military Procurement Expenditures (t-2) to Military Procurement Expenditures (t-1) to State Income (t); and House Dem on Committee (t-3) to Military Procurement Expenditures (t-2) to State Income (t-1) to State Income (t). Thus the calculation is (.031 × .025 + .691 × .031 × .025 + .031 × .809 × .025 + .031 × .025 × .939) ÷ .025 = .1066, or about 10.7 percent.

4. This is an assumption we cannot test because of the difficulties in estimating models of committee representation that distinguish between parties described in chapter 4.

CHAPTER 10

1. See Appendix B.

2. Research following this approach, incidentally, leads to another distributive anomaly. Alvarez and Saving (1997) and Rundquist, Lee, and Luor (1995) report that committee members' constituencies benefit disproportionately from the distribution of Medicare, Medicaid, and Social Security expenditures. Thus there appears to be benefit targeting of the type predicted by distributive theory for programs that Lowi's and Wilson's approaches would treat as redistributive.

APPENDIX A

1. Both the House and Senate committee representation variables for the period covered have about 56 percent of the observations coded as 1 and 44 percent coded as 0.

2. This has been our basic approach in previous work as well (Carsey and Rundquist 1999a, 1999b).

REFERENCES

Adler, Scott E. 1999. "Protecting Turf in a Reform Era: Distributive Politics and Congressional Committee Reform in the 93rd Congress." Paper presented at the annual meeting of the Midwest Political Science Association, Chicago.

Adler, Scott E., and John Lapinski. 1997. "Demand-Side Theory and Congressional Committee Composition: A Constituency Characteristics Approach." *American Journal of Political Science* 41: 895–918.

Aldrich, John H. 1995. *Why Parties? The Origin and Transformation of Party Politics in America.* Chicago: University of Chicago Press.

Alesina, Alberto, and Dani Rodrik. 1994. "Distributive Politics and Economic Growth." *Quarterly Journal of Economics* 109: 465–90.

Alvarez, R. M., and J. L. Saving. 1997. "Congressional Committees and the Political Economy of Federal Outlays." *Public Choice* 92: 55–73.

Anton, Thomas J., Jerry P. Hawley, and Kevin L. Kramer. 1980. *Moving Money: An Empirical Analysis of Federal Expenditure Patterns.* Cambridge, Mass.: Oelgeschlager, Gunn, and Hain.

Arnold, R. Douglas. 1979. *Congress and the Bureaucracy.* New Haven: Yale University Press.

———. 1990. *The Logic of Congressional Action.* New Haven: Yale University Press.

Arrow, Kenneth. 1951. *Collective Choice and Individual Values.* 2d ed. New Haven: Yale University Press.

Baron, David P., and John Ferejohn. 1989. "Bargaining in Legislatures," *American Political Science Review,* 83, no. 4 (December): 1181–1206.

Bartels, Larry. 1991. "Constituency Opinion and Congressional Policy Making: The Reagan Defense Buildup." *American Political Science Review* 85: 457–74.

Baumgartner, Frank R., and Bryan D. Jones. 1993. *Agendas and Instability in American Politics.* Chicago: University of Chicago Press.

Beck, Nathaniel, and Jonathan Katz. 1995. "What to Do 'and Not to Do' with Time-Series Cross-Section Data." *American Political Science Review* 89: 634–47.

Bernstein, Robert A., and William W. Anthony. 1974. "The ABM Issue in the Senate, 1968–70: The Importance of Ideology." *American Political Science Review* 68: 1198–1206.

Bickers, Kenneth, Patrick Sellers, and Robert Stein. 1996. "The Bi-Partisan Pork Barrel." Paper presented at the annual meeting of the American Political Science Association, San Francisco.

Bickers, Kenneth, and Robert Stein. 1991. *Federal Domestic Outlays, 1983 to 1990: A Data Book.* Armonk, N.Y.: M. E. Sharpe.

———. 1996. "The Electoral Dynamics of the Federal Pork Barrel." *American Journal of Political Science* 40: 1300–1326.

———. 1999. "The Congressional Pork Barrel in a Republican Era." Paper prepared for the annual meeting of the Midwest Political Science Association, Chicago.

Black, Duncan. 1958. *Theory of Committees and Elections.* London: Cambridge University Press.

Bollen, Kenneth A. 1989. *Structural Equations with Latent Variables.* New York: Wiley.

Brace, Paul. 1993. *State Government and Economic Performance.* Baltimore: Johns Hopkins University Press.

Brown, Robert D. 1995. "Party Cleavages and Welfare Effort in the American States." *American Political Science Review* 89: 23–33.

Browne, M. W., and G. Arminger. 1995. "Specification and Estimation of Mean- and Covariance-Structure Models." In G. Arminger, C. C. Clogg, and M. E. Sobel, eds., *Handbook of Statistical Modeling for the Social and Behavioral Sciences,* 185–250. New York: Plenum Press.

Cain, Bruce, John Ferejohn, and Morris Fiorina. 1987. *The Personal Vote: Constituency Service and Electoral Independence.* Cambridge, Mass.: Harvard University Press.

Campbell, Angus, Phillip E. Converse, Warren E. Miller, and Donald E. Stokes. 1960. *The American Voter.* New York: Wiley.

Carsey, Thomas M. 2000. *Campaign Dynamics: The Race for Governor.* Ann Arbor: University of Michigan Press.

Carsey, Thomas M. and Barry S. Rundquist. 1999a. "Party and Committee in Congressional Policy Making: Evidence from the Domestic Distribution of Defense Expenditures." *Journal of Politics* 61: 1156–69.

———. 1999b. "The Reciprocal Relationship between State Defense Interest and Committee Representation in Congress." *Public Choice* 99: 455–63.

Carsey, Thomas M., Barry Rundquist, and Sharon Fox. 1997. "Defense Spending and Economic Development in the American States." Paper presented at the annual meeting of the Midwest Political Science Association, Chicago.

Collie, Melissa. 1988. "The Legislature and Distributive Policy Making in Formal Perspective." *Legislative Studies Quarterly* 13: 427–458.

Cox, Gary W., and Mathew D. McCubbins. 1993. *Legislative Leviathan.* Berkeley: University of California Press.

Crump, Jeffrey, and Clark Archer. 1993. "Spatial and Temporal Variability in the Geography of American Defense Outlays." *Political Geography* 12, (1): 38–63.

Dawson, John, and Peter Stan. 1995. *Public Expenditures in the United States: 1952–1993.* Santa Monica, Calif.: RAND Corporation.

Deckard, Barbara. 1972. "State Party Delegations in the U.S. House of Representatives: A Comparative Study." *Journal of Politics*, 35, no. 3 (February): 199–222.

Dering, Robert S. 1998. "The Politics of Military Base Closures." Paper presented at the annual meeting of the American Political Science Association, New York.

Downs, Anthony. 1957. *An Economic Theory of Democracy.* New York: Harper and Row.

Elazar, Daniel. 1984. *American Federalism: A View from the States.* 3d ed. New York: Harper and Row.

Erickson, Robert, Gerald Wright, and John McIver. 1993. *Statehouse Democracy.* New York: Cambridge University Press.

Feldman, Paul, and James Jondrow. 1984. "Congressional Elections and Local Federal Spending." *American Journal of Political Science* 28: 147–64.

Fenno, Richard A. 1973. "The Internal Distribution of Influence: The House." In David Truman, ed., *Congress and America's Future.* 2d ed., 63–90. Englewood Cliffs, NJ: Prentice-Hall.

———. 1978. *Homestyle.* Boston: Little, Brown.

Ferejohn, John A. 1974. *Pork Barrel Politics: Rivers and Harbors Legislation, 1947–1968.* Stanford: Stanford University Press.

Finkel, Steven. 1995. *Causal Analysis with Panel Data*. Thousand Oaks, Calif.: Sage.

Fiorina, Morris P. 1977. *Congress: Keystone of the Washington Establishment*. New Haven: Yale University Press.

———. 1981. "Universalism, Reciprocity, and Distributive Policy Making in Majority Rule Institutions." in John P. Crecine, ed., *Research in Public Policy Making and Management*, 1: 193–221. Greenwich, Conn.: JAI Press.

Fleisher, Richard. 1985. "Economic Benefit, Ideology, and Senate Voting on the B-1 Bomber." *American Politics Quarterly* 13: 200–11.

Gansler, Jacques S. 1981. *The Defense Industry*. Cambridge, Mass.: MIT Press.

Goodwin, George, Jr. 1970. *The Little Legislatures*. Amherst: University of Massachusetts Press.

Goss, Carol. 1972. "Military Committee Membership and Defense Related Benefits." *Western Political Quarterly* 25: 216–33.

Hall, Richard L. 1996. *Participation in Congress*. New Haven: Yale University Press.

Hansen, Susan. 1993. "State Policies and Economic Development: Lessons and Caveats for the Clinton Administration." Paper presented at the conference State Economic Development Policy, Institute of Government and Public Affairs, University of Illinois at Chicago.

Heitshusen, Valerie. 1991. "Do Committee Members Get a Bigger Piece of the Pie? The Distribution of Program Expenditures to Members of Congress in the 1980s." Paper presented at the annual meeting of the American Political Science Association, Chicago.

Hinich, Melvin J., and Michael C. Munger. 1994. *Ideology and the Theory of Political Choice*. Ann Arbor: University of Michigan Press.

Hinkley, Barbara. 1971. "Policy Content, Committee Membership, and Behavior." *American Journal of Political Science* 19: 543–58.

———. 1975. "Policy Content, Committee Membership, and Behavior." *American Journal of Political Science* 19: 543–57.

Hird, John. 1991. "The Political Economy of Pork: Project Selection in the U.S. Corp of Engineers." *American Political Science Review* 85: 429–56.

Hsiao, Cheng. 1986. *Analysis of Panel Data*. New York: Cambridge University Press.

Huntington, Samuel P. 1961. *The Common Defense*. Cambridge, Mass.: Harvard University Press.

Jaccard, James, Robert Turrisi, and Choi K. Wan. 1990. *Interaction Effects in Multiple Regression*. Thousand Oaks, Calif.: Sage.

Jackson, John E., and John Kingdon. 1992. "Ideology, Interest Group Ratings, and Legislative Votes." *American Journal of Political Science* 19: 851–80.

Jackson, Robert, and Thomas M. Carsey. 1999a. "Group Components of Presidential Voting across the U.S. States." *Political Behavior* 21: 123–51.

———. 1999b. "Presidential Voting across the American States." *American Politics Quarterly* 27: 379–402.

Kalt, Joseph P., and Mark A. Zupan. 1990. "The Apparent Ideological Behavior of Legislators: Testing for Principle-Agent Slack in Political Institutions." *Journal of Political Economy* 33: 103–31.

Kau, James B., and Paul H. Rubin. 1982. *Congressmen, Constituents, and Contributors: Determinants of Roll Call Voting in the House of Representatives.* Boston: Martinus Nijhoff.

Kaufman, William W. 1992. *Assessing the Base Force: How Much Is Too Much?* Studies in Defense Policy. Washington, D.C.: Institution.

King, Gary, Robert O. Keohane, and Sidney Verba. 1994. *Designing Social Inquiry.* Princeton: Princeton University Press.

Krehbiel, Keith. 1991. *Information and Legislative Organization.* Ann Arbor: University of Michigan Press.

———. 1998. *Pivotal Politics.* Chicago: University of Chicago Press.

Levitt, Steven D., and James M. Poterba. 1994. "Congressional Distributive Politics and State Economic Performance." NBER Working Papers No. 4721. National Bureau of Economic Research.

Levitt, Steven D., and James M. Snyder. 1995. "Political Parties and the Distribution of Federal Outlays." *American Journal of Political Science* 39: 958–80.

———. 1997. "The Impact of Federal Spending on House Election Outcomes." *Journal of Political Economy* 105, no. 1 (February): 30–53.

Lindsay, James. 1990. "Congress and the Defense Budget: Parochialism or Policy." In Robert Higgs, ed., *Arms Politics and the Economy*, 174–201. New York: Homes and Meier.

———. 1991. *Congress and Nuclear Weapons.* Baltimore: Johns Hopkins University Press.

Lowi, Theodore. 1964. "American Business, Public Policy, Case Studies, and Political Theory." *World Politics* 16 (July): 677–715.

Luor, Ching-Jyuhn. 1995. "United States Distributive Politics in the 1980s." Ph.D. dissertation, University of Illinois at Chicago.

McGinnis, Michael and John Williams. 2001. *Compound Dilemmas: Democracy, Collective Action, and Superpower Rivalry.* Ann Arbor: University of Michigan Press.

McKelvey, R. D. 1975. "Policy Related Voting and Electoral Equilibrium." *Econometrica* 43: 685–843.

Markusen, Ann, P. Hall, S. Campbell, and S. Diedrich. 1991. *The Rise of the Gunbelt.* London: Oxford University Press.

Mayer, Kenneth. 1991. *The Politics of Military Procurement.* New Haven: Yale University Press.

Mayhew, David R. 1974. *Congress: The Electoral Connection.* New Haven: Yale University Press.

Miranda, Rowan, and Ittipone Tunyavong. 1994. "Patterned Inequality? Reexamining the Role of Distributive Politics in Urban Service Delivery." *Urban Affairs Quarterly* 29, no. 4 (June): 509–34.

Moyer, Wayne. 1973. "House Voting on Defense: An Ideological Explanation." In Bruce Russett and Alfred Stepan, eds., *Military Force and American Society,* 106–42. New York: Harper and Row.

Mueller, Dennis. 1989. *Public Choice.* 2d ed. New York: Cambridge University Press.

Niou, Emerson M. S., and Peter C. Ordeshook. 1985. "Universalism in Congress." *American Journal of Political Science* 29: 246–58.

Peck, Merton J., and Frederick M. Scherer. 1962. *The Weapons Acquisition Process: An Economic Analysis.* Boston: Division of Research, Graduate School of Business Administration, Harvard University.

Peterson, Paul E. 1995. *The Price of Federalism.* New York: Brookings Institution.

Plott, Charles. 1967. "Some Organizational Influences on Urban Renewal Decisions." *American Economic Review* 63 (May): 306–21.

Poole, Keith, and Howard Rosenthal. 1997. *Congress: A Political-Economic History of Roll Call Voting.* New York: Oxford University Press.

Ray, Bruce A. 1980a. "Congressional Promotion of District Interests: Does Power on the Hill Really Make a Difference?" In Barry Rundquist, ed., *Political Benefits: Empirical Studies of American Public Programs,* 1–36. Lexington, Mass.: D. C. Heath.

———. 1980b. "Federal Spending and the Selection of Committee Assignments in the U.S. House of Representatives." *American Journal of Political Science* 24: 494–510.

———. 1980c. "The Responsiveness of the U.S. Congressional Armed Services Committees to Their Parent Bodies." *Legislative Studies Quarterly* 5 (4): 501–16.

———. 1981. "Military Committee Membership in the House of Representatives and the Allocation of Defense Department Outlays." *Western Political Quarterly* 34: 222–34.

————. 1982. "Causation in the Relationship Between Congressional Position and Federal Spending." *Polity* 24: 676–90.

Rhee, Jungho. 1994. "Statistical Models of Congress and Defense Spending, 1965–1983." Ph.D. dissertation, University of Illinois at Chicago.

Riker, William. 1962. *The Theory of Political Coalitions*. New Haven: Yale University Press.

————. 1980. "Implications from the Disequilibrium of Majority Rule for the Study of Institutions." *American Political Science Review* 74: 432–46.

————. 1990. "Heresthetic and Rhetoric in the Spatial Model." In James M. Enclow and Melvin J. Hinich, eds., *Advances in the Spatial Theory of Voting*, 46–65. Cambridge: Cambridge University Press.

Rohde, David W. 1991. *Parties and Leaders in the Post-Reform House*. Chicago: University of Chicago Press.

Rohde, David, and Kenneth Shepsle. 1973. "Democratic Committee Assignments in the House of Representatives: Strategic Aspects of a Social Choice Process." *American Political Science Review* 67: 889–905.

Rundquist, Barry, Thomas M. Carsey, Lisa Schmit, and Jungho Rhee. 1997. "Congressional Committees and Interest Representation in Defense Contracting." Paper presented at the annual meeting of the Midwest Political Science Association, Chicago.

Rundquist, Barry, and John Ferejohn. 1975. "Observations on a Distributive Theory of Policy Making: Two American Expenditure Programs Compared." In Craig Liske, William Loehr, and John McCamant, eds., *Comparative Public Policy: Issues, Theories, and Methods*, 87–108. New York: Wiley.

Rundquist, Barry, Jeong-Hwa Lee, and Ching-Jyuhn Luor. 1995. "States vs. Districts as Units of Analysis in Distributive Studies: An Exploration."Paper presented at the annual meeting of the Midwest Political Science Association, Chicago.

Rundquist, Barry, Jeong-Hwa Lee, and Jungho Rhee. 1994. "Reexamining Distributive Theories in the Light of Bickers and Stein's Data Book." Paper presented at the annual meeting of the Midwest Political Science Association, Chicago.

————. 1996. "The Distributive Politics of Cold War Defense Spending: Some State Level Evidence." *Legislative Studies Quarterly* 21: 265–82.

Rundquist, Barry, Jeong-Hwa Lee, Jungho Rhee, and Sharon Fox. 1997. "Modeling State Representation on Defense Committees in Congress, 1959–1989." *American Politics Quarterly* 25: 35–55.

Rundquist, Barry, Uma Sharma, Gerald Strom, Sandy Yeh, and Jungho Rhee. 1993. "Congress and Military-Industrial Relations: Exploring the

Subcontractor Problem." Paper presented at the annual meeting of the Midwest Political Science Association, Chicago.

Russett, Bruce. 1970. *What Price Vigilance?* New Haven: Yale University Press.

Sandler, Todd, and Keith Hartley. 1995. *The Economics of Defense.* Cambridge: Cambridge University press.

Sapolsky, Harvey. 1972. *The Polaris System Development.* Cambridge, Mass.: Harvard University Press.

Schmit, Lisa. 1998. "The Missing Link: The Relationship between Defense Expenditures and Electoral Outcomes." Paper presented at the annual meeting of the Midwest Political Science Association, Chicago.

———. 2000. "The Electoral Connection and Defense Contracting," Ph.D. dissertation, University of Illinois at Chicago.

Shepsle, Kenneth. 1978. *The Giant Gigsaw Puzzle: Democratic Committee Assignments in the Modern House.* Chicago: University of Chicago Press.

———. 1979. "Institutional Arrangements and Equilibrium in Multidimensional Voting Models." *American Journal of Political Science* 32: 27–59.

Shepsle, Kenneth A., and Mark S. Bonchek. 1997. *Analyzing Politics.* New York: W. W. Norton.

Shepsle, Kenneth A., and Barry R. Weingast. 1981. "Structure Induced Equilibrium and Legislative Choice." *Public Choice* 37: 503–19.

———. 1987. "The Institutional Foundations of Committee Power." *American Political Science Review* 81: 85–104.

———. 1989. "Political Preferences for the Pork Barrel." *American Journal of Political Science* 25: 96–111.

———. 1995. "Positive Theories of Congressional Institutions." In Kenneth Shepsle and Barry Weingast, eds., *Positive Theories of Congressional Institutions,* 5–36. Ann Arbor: Michigan University Press.

Soherr-Hadwiger, David. 1998. "Military Construction Policy: A Test of Competing Explanations of Universalism in Congress." *Legislative Studies Quarterly* 23 no. 1 (February): 57–78.

Stein, Robert, and Kenneth Bickers. 1994. "Universalism and the Electoral Connection: A Test and Some Doubts." *Political Research Quarterly* 47: 295–317.

———. 1997. *Perpetuating the Pork Barrel: Policy Subsystems and American Democracy.* New York: Cambridge University Press.

Stimson, James A. 1985. "Regression in Space and Time: A Statistical Essay." *American Journal of Political Science* 25: 914–47.

Sundstrom, Frances. 1996. "State Representation and Public Policy: The Consequences of the Geographic Distribution of Federal Domestic

Assistance." Paper presented at the annual meeting of the Midwest Political Science Association, Chicago.

Trubowitz, Peter. 1998. *Defining the National Interest: Conflict and Change in American Foreign Policy.* Chicago: University of Chicago Press.

Tullock, Gordon. 1981. "Why So Much Stability?" *Public Choice* 37, (2): 189–202.

———. 1998. *On Voting: A Public Choice Approach.* Northampton, Mass.: Edward Elgar.

U.S. Department of Defense. *Prime Contract Awards by State and Region, 1959 to 1989* [and other years]. Office of the Secretary of Defense.

U.S. General Accounting Office. 1998a. "Defense Spending and Employment: Information Limitations Impede Thorough Assessments." (Letter Report, 01/14/98, GAO/NSIAD-98-57.)

———. 1998b. GAO NSIAD-98-139R. New Mexico Federal Expenditures.

U.S. House Journal. Various Congresses. Washington, D.C.: Government Printing Office.

Van der Slik, Jack R. 1995. *One for All and All for Illinois.* Springfield, Ill.: Sangamon State University.

Weingast, Barry R. 1979. "A Rational Choice Perspective on Congressional Norms." *American Journal of Political Science* 23: 245–62.

———. 1994. "Reflections on Distributive Politics and Universalism." *Political Research Quarterly* 47: 319–27.

Weingast, Barry R., and William Marshall. 1988. "The Industrial Organization of Congress, or Why Legislatures, Like Firms, Are Not Organized as Markets." *Journal of Political Economy* 96: 132–63.

Weingast, Barry R., Kenneth A. Shepsle, and Christopher Johnson. 1981. "The Political Economy of Benefits and Costs: A Neo-classical Approach to Distributive Politics." *Journal of Political Economy* 83: 914–27.

Wilson, James Q. 1973. *Political Organizations.* New York: Basic Books.

Wittman, Donald. 1995. *The Myth of Democratic Failure.* Chicago: University of Chicago Press.

Wolf, Charles, Jr. 1988. *Markets or Governments: Choosing between Imperfect Alternatives.* Cambridge, Mass.: MIT Press.

INDEX